MENLO SCHOOL
· MENLO COLLEGE ·
founded 1915

Gift of

HYMAN JEBB LEVY
FOUNDATION

Who Were the Israelites?

Sven Ahlström
In Memoriam

Who Were
the Israelites?

by

Gösta W. Ahlström

EISENBRAUNS
Winona Lake, IN
1986

Library of Congress Cataloging-in-Publication Data

Ahlström, Gösta W. (Gösta Werner), 1918–
  Who were the Israelites?

  Includes bibliographical references and indexes.
  1. Israel—Name. 2. Ethnology—Palestine. 3. Bible. O.T.—
Historiography. I. Title.
BM729.N3A35   1986   913.3'0014   86-8932
ISBN 0-931464-24-2

Contents

Foreword

The present investigation is concerned with the origin and history of the name *Israel*. I maintain that the name originally denoted a territory, and that the people who settled in it became known as Israelites. The changes in the use of the name and its meaning are then traced down to the Persian period and the emergence of Judaism. As a result, I conclude that the name Israel was used in three ways in biblical writings: as a territorial designation, as a national name, and as an ideological characterization. Originally, the name was a label for all peoples of a certain territory irrespective of ethnicity, but later it became a national designation, and eventually it became a term restricted to those who embraced Ezra's law. Thus, the name Israel evolved into an exclusive designation for the people of Yahweh and, as such, became a synonym for Judaism.

I wish to express my deep gratitude to Mrs. Diana Edelman for her excellent assistance with compositional problems (especially related to English) and for retyping the manuscript.

G. W. Ahlström
Chicago, July, 1984

Abbreviations

AASOR	Annual of the American Schools of Oriental Research
AfO	*Archiv für Orientforschung*
ANET	*Ancient Near Eastern Texts Relating to the Old Testament*, ed. J. B. Pritchard
AOAT	Alter Orient und Altes Testament
AOS	American Oriental Series
BA	*Biblical Archaeologist*
BAR	*Biblical Archaeology Review*
BASOR	*Bulletin of the American Schools of Oriental Research*
BBB	Bonner biblische Beiträge
BKAT	Biblischer Kommentar: Altes Testament
BZAW	Beiheft zur Zeitschrift für die alttestamentliche Wissenschaft
CAD	*The Assyrian Dictionary of the Oriental Institute of the University of Chicago*
CAH	*Cambridge Ancient History*
CBQ	*Catholic Biblical Quarterly*
ConB	Coniectanea biblica
DTT	*Dansk teologisk tidsskrift*
EA	El-Amarna
EB	Early Bronze
EAEHL	*Encyclopedia of Archaeological Excavations in the Holy Land*
HAT	Handbuch zum Alten Testament
HUCA	*Hebrew Union College Annual*
IDB	*Interpreter's Dictionary of the Bible*
ICC	International Critical Commentary
IEJ	*Israel Exploration Journal*
JAOS	*Journal of the American Oriental Society*
JBL	*Journal of Biblical Literature*

JEA   *Journal of Egyptian Archaeology*
JESHO   *Journal of the Economic and Social History of the Orient*
JPOS   *Journal of the Palestine Oriental Society*
JSOT   *Journal for the Study of the Old Testament*
JSS   *Journal of Semitic Studies*
JTC   *Journal for Theology and the Church*
JTS   *Journal of Theological Studies*
KS   A. Alt, *Kleine Schriften*
LB   Late Bronze
MANE   Monographs of the Ancient Near East
MB   Middle Bronze
OIP   Oriental Institute Publications
OLZ   *Orientalische Literaturzeitung*
PEQ   *Palestine Exploration Quarterly*
RA   *Revue d'assyriologie et d'archéologie orientale*
RB   *Revue biblique*
SAOC   Studies in Ancient Oriental Civilization
SBL   Society of Biblical Literature
SBT   Studies in Biblical Theology
SNVAO   Skrifter utgitt av Det Norske Videnskaps-Akademi i
        Oslo
SPDS   *Studies in the Period of David and Solomon*, ed. T. Ishida
StTH   *Studia theologica*
TWAT   *Theologisches Wörterbuch zum Alten Testament*, ed. G. J.
        Botterweck and H. Ringgren
UF   *Ugarit-Forschungen*
UUÅ   *Uppsala Universitets Årsskrift*
VT   *Vetus Testamentum*
VTSup   Vetus Testamentum, Supplements
ZA   *Zeitschrift für Assyriologie*
ZAW   *Zeitschrift für die alttestamentliche Wissenschaft*
ZDPV   *Zeitschrift des deutschen Palästina-Vereins*

1

Introduction

Palestine is a land of geographical contrasts and always has
been, with its mountainous regions of rolling or steep,
barren hills, its fertile valleys and lowlands, and its dunes
and deserts. The Jordan valley is below sea level, and the
Dead Sea is 1284 feet (ca. 396 m.) below the Mediterranean
Sea. By contrast, the highest mountain in western Galilee,
Jebel Jarmaq (Har Meron), reaches a height of 3963 feet
(1208 m.). In the central mountain areas, the highest point
is located at biblical Baal Hazor (Tell ʿAṣur) with an eleva-
tion of 3333 feet (1016 m.).[1]

With these differences in mind, it is understandable that
the demographic picture is diverse. The mountainous areas
were not as heavily populated as the lowlands and the
coastal area; in fact, the hills were only sparsely populated.
This is an important consideration in discussing the origin
of the Israelites, a people which reputedly inhabited the
central hill country of Palestine.

In order to situate the Israelites in history, we must deal
with both the literary and the archaeological sources. The
literary material mainly consists of the texts of the Hebrew
Bible. The only non-biblical text from the pre-monarchic
period which refers to Israel is Merneptah's Stela, which is
sometimes called the Israel Stela.[2] In addition to this text,

---

[1] For the country's geography, see D. Baly, *The Geography of the Bible*
(New York and London, 1974) 28–42; E. Orni and E. Efrat, *Geography of
Israel* (3rd ed., Jerusalem, 1971) 3ff.; Y. Aharoni, *The Land of the Bible* (2nd
ed., Philadelphia, 1979) 21ff.

[2] For the text, see *ANET*, 378.

the Amarna Letters are a source for reconstructing the political and social milieu in Palestine in the period before the emergence of Israel.

While archaeological material does not explicitly tell us anything about the origin of the Israelites, it can provide us with information about the settlement patterns and cultural traits of the people living in Palestine during the period in which Israel appeared in history. Because the biblical textual material is a product of faith, its goal is not primarily to report and preserve historical facts and thus a harmonization between the biblical text and the archaeological remains cannot always be made. However, archaeology is a valuable tool for evaluating textual information: it can confirm the picture given by the biblical writers, correct it on many points, or give an entirely different scenario.

An excellent example of the relation between the biblical text and archaeology is the so-called "conquest tradition" in the Book of Joshua. As will be seen, archaeology does not support the Bible's claim that a conquest led to the emergence of an Israelite society and kingdom in Canaan.[3] The conquest story must be understood from an ideological point of view. As will be mentioned below, the Joshua narrative advocates the people's right to the land at a time when their claim to the land was disputed. Therefore, both the promise of the land (Gen 12:1f.) and the conquest were set back into antiquity to serve as a precedent.

Archaeology does not support the view[4] that there was a well-organized military conquest of Canaan with a consequent destruction of the main urban centers, as a majority

---

[3] See my discussion in "Another Moses Tradition," *JNES* 39 (1980) 65ff.

[4] See, for instance, the discussions of M. Noth, "Der Beitrag der Archäologie zur Geschichte Israels," (VTSup 7; Leiden, 1960) 262ff.; J. B. Pritchard, "Culture and History," in *The Bible in Modern Scholarship* (ed. J. P. Hyatt; Nashville and New York, 1965) 319ff.; R. de Vaux, "On Right and Wrong Uses of Archaeology," in *Near Eastern Archaeology in the Twentieth Century* (ed. J. A. Sandars; Garden City, NY, 1970) 64ff.; and M. Weippert, *The Settlement of the Israelite Tribes in Palestine* (SBT 2nd Series 21; London, 1971) 128ff.

of scholars have advocated. The destruction layers found at ruined sites from the 13th century B.C. are mainly to be attributed to Egyptian campaigns and the Sea Peoples. Other contributing factors could have been feuding between different parts of the population or between city-states and accidents, such as fires. Archaeology tends to indicate that there was a much greater continuity in the material cultures of the Late Bronze and Iron I periods than is usually assumed by advocates of the conquest model.[5]

Restlessness was not a new phenomenon at the end of the 13th century B.C. Military rule and political domination by non-indigenous powers had always created distress and disturbances. The so-called "Amarna period" in Syria-Palestine (14th century B.C.), for example, was a period of internal feuding between city rulers and of disturbances by uprooted peoples and outcasts.[6] Behind all of this there was the greater political arena and the power struggle between Egypt, Mitanni, and the Hittites for the domination of Syria.[7] In this struggle, Egypt's power declined steadily, as did Mitanni's. Shuppiluliuma's Second Syrian War (ca. 1325–1319) resulted in the collapse of the Mitanni kingdom,

---

[5] See, for instance, Ruth Amiran, *Ancient Pottery of the Holy Land* (Jerusalem, 1969) 192; K. M. Kenyon, *Amorites and Canaanites* (London, 1966) 77; and Y. Aharoni, *Land of the Bible* (2nd ed rev. A. F. Rainey; Philadelphia, 1979) 240. In spite of this, he still speaks of the "unique nature" of the Israelites and their occupation of Israel.

[6] For the letters from Tell el-Amarna, see J. A. Knudtzon, *Die el-Amarna Tafeln* (2 vols.; Leipzig, 1915; reprinted, Aalen, 1964); A. F. Rainey, *El Amarna Tablets 359–379: Supplement to J. A. Knutzon, Die el-Amarna Tafeln* (AOAT 8; Neukirchen-Vluyn, 1970). For an English translation, see S. A. B. Mercer, *The Tell el-Amarna Tablets* (2 vols.; Toronto, 1939); and for a review, W. F. Albright, "The Amarna Letters from Palestine," *CAH*[3] II/2 (Cambridge, 1975) 98–116. For the chronology, see, among others, E. F. Campbell, *The Chronology of the Amarna Letters* (Baltimore, 1964) and C. Kühne, *Die Chronologie der internationalen Korrespondenz von El-Amarna* (AOAT 17; Neukirchen-Vluyn, 1973).

[7] For the political picture in Palestine during the 14th century B.C., see M. W. Several, "Reconsidering the Egyptian Empire in Palestine during the Amarna Period," *PEQ* 104 (1972) 123ff. He states that the Amarna letters have "erroneously been interpreted as documenting imperial decline in Palestine" (p. 123).

and most of its territory and its Syrian vassals came under Hittite rule.[8]

In the Late Bronze period Canaan was dominated by Egypt. There were several Egyptian strongholds in the Sinai and in the coastal area of southern Canaan. Administrative centers and garrison cities were located, for instance, at Gaza, Joppa, and Beth-Shan,[9] and there was a "government house" at Aphek, which is dated from the time of Ramses II.[10]

Outside of the important coastal area with its trade routes, Canaan was not of much interest to the Egyptians since it was poor in raw materials, wealthy cities, and agricultural produce. In particular, the mountain region was of minor political importance since it had only a few people, few fortified cities, and a general lack of urban culture. Egyptian control over the country was generally oppressive and impoverishing and eliminated all incentives for the flowering of cultural life, even in the old urban centers. (The hills, by their very nature, were not conducive to the development of urban culture.) According to W. F. Albright and others, the Late Bronze culture of

[8] For the events of this period, see W. Helck, *Die Beziehungen Ägyptens zu Vorderasien im 3. und 2. Jahrtausend v. Chr.* (2nd ed., Wiesbaden, 1971) 168–88; H. Klengel, *Geschichte und Kultur Altsyriens* (Vienna and Munich, 1979) 75–85; A. Goetze, "The Struggle for the Domination of Syria (1400–1300 B.C.)," *CAH³* II/2 (Cambridge, 1975) 1–10; and A. Goetze, "The Hittites and Syria (1300–1200 B.C.)," *CAH³* II/2 (Cambridge, 1975) 252–73. Cf. K. A. Kitchen, *Suppiluliuma and the Amarna Pharaohs* (Liverpool, 1962). The chronology is based upon that developed by E. F. Wente and C. van Siclen, "A Chronology of the New Kingdom," in *Studies in Honor of George R. Hughes* (SAOC 39; Chicago, 1976) 217–61.

[9] For the Egyptian administration, see among others, A. Alt, "Die Landnahme der Israeliten in Palästina," *KS* I (Munich, 1953) 97ff. (= "The Settlement of the Israelites in Palestine," in *Essays in Old Testament History and Religion* [Garden City, NY, 1966] 146ff.); Helck, *Die Beziehungen*, 246ff.; my book, *Royal Administration and National Religion in Ancient Palestine* (Studies in the History of the Ancient Near East 1; Leiden, 1982) 10ff.; and J. M. Weinstein, "The Egyptian Empire in Palestine: A Reassessment," *BASOR* 241 (1981) 17ff.

[10] M. Kochavi, "Canaanite Aphek: Its Acropolis and Inscriptions," *Expedition* 20 (1978) 12–17 and "The History and Archaeology of Aphek-Antipatris: Biblical City in the Sharon Plain," *BA* 44 (1981) 75–86.

southern Canaan was decreasing "rather steadily" and reached its low point sometime during the latter part of the 13th century B.C.[11] This may be disputed,[12] but Egyptian rule and the many military campaigns through western Palestine may have contributed to a "restless period lacking civil security."[13] This unrest may have increased during the period of the incursions of the Sea Peoples.

It is in this socio-political setting that the first evidence for a people, "Israel," emerging on the historical stage in ancient Palestine, is found. Were the Israelites newcomers to the country or were they indigenous people? Many scholars almost dogmatically accept that the Israelites and Canaanites were two distinctive population groups. The Israelites are thought to have been a semi-nomadic group conquering or infiltrating most of Canaan and, as a people of a culture and religion different from that which was common in Canaan, they clashed quickly with the Canaanites. This reconstruction has been inspired by the Bible's religious (rather than historical) focus on the theological-historical pattern of the "Exodus-Wanderings-Conquest."

Combined with this concern for the origin of Israel as a people has been the search for the origin of the Yahwistic religion. These two questions have been almost impossible to separate in scholarly discussion.[14] They are still interwoven in the most recent treatments of the origin of Israel,

[11] W. F. Albright, *The Archaeology of Palestine* (Gloucester, MA, 1971) 101.

[12] See, for instance, N. Naʾaman, "Economic Aspects of the Egyptian Occupation of Canaan," *IEJ* 31 (1981) 173–85.

[13] Rivka Gonen, "Urban Canaan in the Late Bronze Period," *BASOR* 253 (1984) 70. Ms. Gonen has depicted the Late Bronze Age on the basis of archaeological material only, leaving out of consideration the literary evidence and its bias" (p. 62). She fails to realize that she has in fact accepted the biased biblical evidence when she refers to the "Israelite conquest" of Canaan in her conclusion (p. 70).

[14] A typical example is the assertion of J. L. McKenzie that whenever "there was an Israel there was a Yahweh" ("The Sack of Israel," in *The Quest for the Kingdom of God: Studies in Honor of George E. Mendenhall* [ed. H. B. Huffmon, F. A. Spina, A. R. W. Green; Winona Lake, IN, 1983] 27). The theophoric component ʾēl in the name Israel indicates otherwise.

as for instance, in the writings of G. E. Mendenhall[15] and
N. K. Gottwald.[16] Of these two, only Gottwald considers
the Israelites to have been El worshipers at the very beginning of their history. For both authors, however, Yahweh
was the uniting factor and central power which made
people Israelites. The Yahwistic faith allegedly kept the
"covenantors" together. These covenantors were Canaanite
peasant revolutionaries. Thus, when an Israelite society
first emerged, its religion was Yahwistic. This theory will
be disputed in the following pages.

Mendenhall's basic theory is that there was a wide-scale
peasant revolt in Palestine around 1200 B.C. According to
his proposal, the common people revolted against the city
rulers and then withdrew into the hills to start again,
where they would have been beyond the reach of organized
government. A theory of a withdrawal from the urban and
agricultural/industrial areas of Canaan may be supported
by archaeological material. A specific peasant revolt, on the
other hand, while possible, is not supported by any textual
evidence. The social unrest and upheavals of this period
certainly would have forced some people to escape up to
the hills and this could have been the reason for the many
new settlements in the hill country which can be dated to
this period. The move to the hills seems to have been due
to discontent with the urban societies and a desire to escape
the devastating wars which were so frequent in western
Palestine.[17]

---

[15] G. Mendenhall, "The Hebrew Conquest of Palestine," *BA* 26 (1962)
66–87, and *The Tenth Generation: The Origin of the Biblical Tradition* (Baltimore, 1973) 122ff.

[16] N. K. Gottwald, *The Tribes of Yahweh: A Sociology of the Religion of
Liberated Israel, 1250–1050 B.C.E.* (Maryknoll, NY, 1979).

[17] M. L. Chaney has maintained that while "comparative studies
cannot prove that ancient Israel emerged from a Palestinian peasant's
revolt, they can allow us to determine whether there existed in Late
Bronze and early Iron I Palestine a concatenation of conditions which in
other agrarian societies have proved conducive to broader peasant re-
volts" ("Ancient Palestinian Peasant Movements and the Formation of
Premonarchic Israel," in *Palestine in Transition: The Emergence of Ancient Israel*
[The Social World of Biblical Antiquity Series 2; ed. D. N. Freedman and
D. F. Graf; Sheffield, 1983] 61). Chaney has shown that the possibility

A withdrawal of this kind, however, is not the same as a revolution. Although the people abandoned the Canaanite societies, they took with them the culture and religion which they had always known and retained them in their new settlements. With this in mind, Mendenhall's thesis that Yahweh was a god of the newly emerged Israel becomes rather questionable, not to say unrealistic. How can one maintain that peoples from different areas in Canaan could all have had Yahweh as their main god or could have accepted him to be their chief deity, thus quickly constituting themselves as biblical "Israelites?" The very name Israel itself also contradicts Mendenhall's proposal since it shows that the people's main god was the head of the Canaanite pantheon, El.

How were all of these escapees from the cultural and industrial areas of Canaan able to "find" Yahweh in the unsettled places of the hills where they built their settlements? Why would they have been associated with a deity from Edom? The biblical tradition mentions that Yahweh came from Seir, Paran, and Teman, which are all biblical names for Edomite territories (Deut 33:2; Judg 5:4; Hab 3:3). The association of Yahweh with the south in these three independent traditions strongly suggests that this is a genuine association. Yahweh's Edomite "origin" has now been confirmed by the recovery of the writings of Kuntillet ʿAjrud which mention "Yahweh of Teman and his Asherah."[18] The literary evidence about Yahweh's southern origin, coupled with the archaeological evidence of the founding of many new settlements in the hills which are characterized mainly by Canaanite cultural remains, allows one to conclude that an Edomite group which worshiped Yahweh was among the many groups of people which

---

existed for a peasant revolt during the LB II–Iron I period, but this is as far as one can go without any firm proof.

[18] See Z. Meshel, "Did Yahweh have a Consort? The New Religious Inscriptions from the Sinai," *BAR* 5 (1979) 24ff.; J. A. Emerton, "New Light on the Israelite Religion: The Implications of the Inscriptions from Kuntillet ʿAjrud," *ZAW* 94 (1982) 2–20; G. W. Ahlström, *An Archaeological Picture of Iron Age Religions in Ancient Palestine* (Studia Orientalia 55/3); Helsinki, 1984) 18ff.

settled in the hill country at this time. However, Yahweh certainly would not have been immediately accepted by all the other groups of the central hills as their main god. The historical process which led to Yahweh becoming the god of all of Canaan is more complex than this.[19]

Mendenhall has theorized further that the so-called "revolutionary"[20] settlers created a theocracy under Yahweh. This theory is incredible not only in light of what has been said above, but it is also illogical according to Mendenhall's own argumentation. Did any of the settlers from the territories of the Canaanite city-states really know anything about Yahweh?[21] Gottwald has avoided this pitfall, acknowledging that the Israelites originally were El worshipers, as the name Israel suggests. He adopts Mendenhall's concept of a Yahwistic theocratic Israel, however, theorizing that when a group escaping from Egypt under the leadership of Moses had settled in Canaan, its god (Yahweh) was accepted through a treaty (covenant) as the deity of the whole Israelite society. This has been concluded from Joshua 24.[22] The Canaanite population of the hills seems to fade away in Gottwald's presentation, but perhaps we should assume that he considers a process of Israelitization to have occurred after the Joshua 24 event at Shechem. Were the people arriving from Egypt Israelites too? Here

[19] Cf. below, p. 92ff.

[20] For a critique of the "peasant revolt" theory, see also A. H. Hauser, "Israel's Conquest of Palestine: A Peasant's Revolt?" *JSOT* 7 (1978) 2–19; cf. N. P. Lemche, "Det revolutionaere Israel," *DTT* 45 (1982) 16–39.

[21] The idea of theocracy had not yet been born. The theocracy known in the Near East was one of the god's rule through his vice-regent, the king. See my *Royal Administration*, 2ff.

[22] Gottwald, *The Tribes of Yahweh*, 564ff. Gottwald has used the amphictyonic hypothesis without accepting the number twelve, although elsewhere he maintains that Saul built up a twelve-tribe militia (p. 367), without any documentation to support his statement. According to Gottwald, Moses does not play any really important role in this early period. He says that "we must come to terms with Moses and the prophets, as with all religious innovators, as propagandists for a religion already formed or forming in a given social field, and thus from the start a thoroughly mixed, diluted, and selected religion" (p. 630).

Gottwald seems to have forgotten that his Israelites were the people leaving the urban societies of Canaan, i.e., Canaanites. Gottwald's historical reconstruction seems to be merely an adaptation of the biblical historiographer's idea that Israel was different from the Canaanites, or, as Gottwald expresses it, "Israel *thought* it was different because it *was* different."[23]

The differences in civilization and culture in Canaan between the peoples of the urban areas on the coast and in the lowlands, on the one hand, and the peoples of the hills, on the other, are well-illustrated by the insights of F. Braudel. He emphasizes the role of geography and environment in the shaping of cultural traits and points to the fact that the "mountains are as a rule worlds apart from civilizations, which are urban and lowland achievement. Their history is to have none, to remain almost on the fringe of the great waves of civilization."[24] Religion is one area in which the mountain civilizations were not as progressive as those in the lowlands. On the whole, the mountain region was more conservative, keeping its own way of life in all respects,[25] and showing some hostility and suspicion toward urban and lowland peoples.[26] These facts should be taken into consideration in a discussion of the political and demographic scene in ancient Palestine around 1200 B.C.

[23] N. K. Gottwald, "Two Models for the Origins of Ancient Israel: Social Revolution or Frontier Development," in *The Quest for the Kingdom of God: Studies in Honor of George E. Mendenhall* (ed. H. B. Huffmon, F. A. Spina, A. R. W. Green; Winona Lake, IN, 1983) 18. He has not yet shown that this Israel was different.

[24] F. Braudel, *The Mediterranean and the Mediterranean World in the Age of Philip II* (2 vols.; New York, Evanston, San Francisco, London, 1972) 1. 34.

[25] Braudel, *The Mediterranean*, 35.

[26] Cf. the Amarna letter EA 292:28–29: *nun-kur-tum iš-tu šadî a-na ia-ši*, "There is hostility in the mountains towards me," said Baᶜlu-shipti (Knudtzon's Addadâni) of Gezer. E. F. Campbell, referring to the collation of the Amarna texts in the British Museum made by W. F. Albright, reads Baᶜlu-šipti for Addadâni (*The Chronology of the Amarna Letters*, 126). For Judges 5 reflecting this kind of hostility, see, for instance, M. Weber, *Ancient Judaism* (tr. H. H. Gerth and D. Martindale; New York, 1952) 54ff.

2
Population Groups and Theories

The available literary material mentions several ethnic and/ or geographical groups in relation to the demographic picture of Palestine in the LB II and Iron I periods. The Bible mentions, for instance, Canaanites, Amorites, Jebusites, Hittites, Hivites, Horites, Gibeonites, Midianites, Kenites, Josephites, Calebites, Jerahmeelites, Danites, Sidonians, etc., in Cisjordan, and in the Transjordan, Arameans, Ammonites, Moabites, and Edomites. The Bible also differentiates peoples by the geographical areas they inhabited. Thus, we find the peoples of Benjamin, Ephraim, Gilead, Asher, Judah, etc. Considering the available non-biblical material from before 1200, which consists mainly of Egyptian inscriptions, we again meet the Canaanites, Asherites,[1] and probably the Danites,[2] and, in addition, the Kharu (Hurrians), the Shasu (or Shosu), the ʿapīru, and a people called Israel.

[1] The earliest reference is in an inscription of Seti I (1291–1272). The name appears again in a list of Ramses II. For the texts, see J. Simons, *Handbook for the Study of Egyptian Topographical Lists Relating to Western Asia* (Leiden, 1937) 147, list 17:4; 162, list 25:8. In Papyrus Anastasi I, 23:6, also dating from the period of Ramses II, Qazardi is named as the ruler of Ahser, which appears to be located in the vicinity of Megiddo. For the text, see Helck, *Die Beziehungen*, 280, n. 24. Gen 30:12 indicates that the Asherites were not originally Israelites, which makes sense in light of these Egyptian texts.

[2] Y. Yadin ("And Dan, Why Did He Abide by the Ships?" *Australian Journal of Archaeology* 1 [1968] 9ff.) has identified the Danites with the Denyen in the Egyptian texts, who participated in the assault on Egypt, and who also were used as mercenaries in the Egyptian forces. E. Oren

The prisoner of war list from the second Syro-Palestinian campaign of Amenhotep II (1453–1419 B.C.) provides a glimpse of the population of Palestine in the 15th century B.C. as seen through Egyptian eyes. Of a total of 101,000 prisoners, 36,300 were Hurrians, 15,200 were Shasu,[3] 3600 were ʿapīru, 640 were Canaanites, 550 were *maryannu* (the chariot nobility), 15,070 were Neges (probably people from Nuḫašši, Syria), and the remaining 30,652 were family members.[4] The majority of the population is considered to have been Hurrian, although this also may be a general designation for the inhabitants of Canaan rather than a true ethnic label. In Egyptian inscriptions, Kharu meant Palestine.[5]

It is useful to try to determine what the term "ʿapīru" signifies in this list. If the Hurrians represent the majority of the population of Palestine, the Neges represent the Syrians and the Shasu represent possibly the "bedouins" of Syria-Palestine, then the rest of the prisoners logically would belong to professional or social categories. This would explain their smaller numbers. The 550 *maryannu* are the chariot nobility. The 640 Canaanites would probably be the (Phoenician) merchants. Since in the Alalakh texts the term ʿapīru sometimes was used for mercenaries,[6] it seems likely that the term is being used in the list of Amenhotep II in the

---

(*The Northern Cemetery of Beth-Shan* [Leiden, 1973] 149f.) has suggested that the so-called "grotesque coffins" at Beth-Shan belonged to Denyen officers.

[3] For the Shasu people located in northern Palestine and southern Syria, see M. Görg, "Thutmosis III und die š3sw-Region," *JNES* 38 (1979) 199–202, and cf. below, pp. 59f.

[4] See Helck, *Die Beziehungen*, 344; Y. Aharoni, *The Land of the Bible* 168; and J. A. Wilson in *ANET*, 246f.

[5] See, for instance, Papyrus Anastasi IIIA, 5f., and cf. R. A. Caminos, *Late Egyptian Miscellanies* (London, 1954) 117. For the Hurrians in Syria-Palestine, see Helck, *Die Beziehungen*, 104, 330f.; and I. J. Gelb, *Hurrians and Subarians* (Chicago, 1944) 67. R. de Vaux, "Les Hurrites de l'histoire et les Horites de la Bible," *RA* 74 (1967) 481–503.

[6] D. J. Wiseman, *The Alalakh Tablets* (London, 1953) texts 180–84. See also the discussion in H. Reviv, "Some Comments on the Maryannu," *IEJ* 22 (1972) 222; R. de Vaux, *The Early History of Israel* (Philadelphia, 1978) 108.

same way to refer to mercenaries in the forces of the Syro-Palestinian city-states.

It is not likely that ʿapīru is used here to designate an ethnic group. The term had a wide semantic range. It could represent a social class,[7] refugees, outcasts, fugitives, rebels, slaves, mercenaries, and sometimes mercenaries with chariots.[8] The term was also applied to robbers and raiders,[9] making it a synonym of Sumerian SA.GAZ and Akkadian ḫabbatu. Finally, ʿapīru could include foreigners or immigrants and thus, would parallel the later Hebrew term *ger*, as R. Borger has pointed out.[10]

The ʿapīru are mentioned frequently in the el-Amarna texts from the 14th century B.C. They appear to have posed a significant threat to the Syro-Palestinian rulers who complained about them as political enemies or hostile peoples close to city-states, rather than as bandits or robbers. The petty princes seem to have labeled as ʿapīru/ḫapiru anyone who was not under the jurisdiction of a city-state, who appeared as a potential enemy or disruptive element, or who opposed a state's policy or ruler.[11] This is evident, for

---

[7] Cf. *CAD* VI (Chicago, 1956) 84.

[8] Wiseman, *The Alalakh Tablets*, texts 180ff. Cf. Säve-Söderbergh, "The ʿprw as Vintagers in Egypt," *Orientalia Suecana* I:1/2 (1952) 5ff.

[9] See among others, J. Bottéro, *Le problème des Ḫabiru* (Cahiers de la Société Asiatique 12; Paris, 1954); M. Greenberg, *The Ḫab/piru* (AOS 39; New Haven, 1955); R. Borger, "Das Problem der ʿapīru ('Ḫabiru')," *ZDPV* 74 (1958) 121–32; J. T. Luke, *Pastoralism and Politics in the Mari Period* (unpub. Ph.D. diss., University of Michigan; Ann Arbor, 1965). G. Buccellati considers them to be politically misplaced persons ("ʿApirû and Munnabtūtu—The Stateless of the First Cosmopolitan Age," *JNES* 36 [1977] 145ff.); cf. J. C. L. Gibson, "Some Important Ethnic Terms in the Pentateuch," *JNES* 20 (1961) 234ff.; M. B. Rowton, "Dimorphic Structure and the Problem of the ʿApiru-ʿIbrîm," *JNES* 35 (1976) 13ff.; and M. Weippert, "Abraham der Hebräer?" *Biblica* 52 (1971) 412ff.

[10] *ZDPV* 74 (1958) 122f. The ʿapīru are also mentioned on a stela of Seti I (1291–1279) from Beth Shan as "of the mountain of Yer. . . ." See A. Rowe, *The Topography and History of Beth-Shan* I (Philadelphia, 1930) 29f., pls. 42–44; cf. J. A. Wilson in *ANET*, 255 and Bottéro, *Le problème des Ḫabiru*, text no. 184. The stele is broken, so little can be learned from it. It is not clear whether ʿapīru is to be seen as an ethnic group or not.

[11] Cf. K. Koch, "Die Hebräer vom Auszug aus Ägypten bis zum Grossreichs Davids," *VT* 19 (1969) 37ff.; J. M. Halligan, "The Role of the

instance, from Amarna Letter EA 74, sent to the pharaoh by Rib-Adda of Byblos, in which the prince states that all the people of his city have gone over to the ᶜapīru (lines 19ff.). It is possible that the people's defection was prompted by their opposition to Rib-Adda's pro-Egyptian stand.[12] It is more likely, though, that it resulted from attempts to Abdi-Ashirta of Amurru to encourage the population of Byblos to rebel against Rib-Adda.[13] Since the Amurru kingdom lay mainly in the mountainous area north and northeast of Byblos, its population probably included refugees, ᶜapīru, alongside the mountain peoples (mainly pastoralists). Abdi-Ashirta would have used these refugees in his military forces, many of whom could have fled from cities and villages ruled by Byblos and other coastal city-states. With this in mind, Rib-Adda's predicament was serious: his enemy Abdi-Ashirta would have been able to use former subjects of Byblos to conquer their old home territories. They knew the city's defense systems well and could persuade old friends to join their cause.[14]

The conflict between Byblos and Amurru must also be seen against the greater political horizon. The Egyptian empire's hold over Syria was threatened by the expansion of the Hittites, and this created turmoil and changes in vassal allegiance. The Hittite incursion not only decreased the Egyptian dominion in southern Syria, but it also reduced the extent of Mitannian rule. Former Egyptian and Mitannian vassals signed treaties with the Hittites. It is in this situation that Abdi-Ashirta of Amurru rose to power and played his

---

Peasant in the Amarna Period," in *Palestine in Transition: The Emergence of Ancient Israel* (The Social World of Biblical Antiquity Series 2; ed. D. N. Freedman and D. F. Graf; Sheffield, 1983) 21f.

[12] Cf. P. Artzi, "'Vox populi' in the el-Amarna Tablets," *RA* 58 (1964) 163ff.

[13] See M. Liverani, "The Politics of Abdi-Ashirta of Amurru" (tr. M. L. Jaffe; MANE 1/5; Malibu, CA 1979) 14–20. He states that Abdi-Ashirta's promises of "peace" to the peasants had "a clearly propagandistic character, having the function of raising hopes and of accentuating the social contrasts, while it would have had hardly any real implementation" (p. 19).

[14] Cf. Liverani, "The Politics of Abdi-Ashirta of Amurru," 16ff.

political game by constantly threatening the coastal cities. The game continued under his son and successor, Aziru.

From the discussion above we conclude that the term ᶜapīru was sometimes used rhetorically to declass one's opponent,[15] even if he belonged to the established social or political structures.[16] The term could therefore include different social categories.[17] In some cases in the Amarna texts, ᶜapīru was used to designate people who had changed their social status or political affiliation.[18] If this category of usage continued into later times, it is possible that the Hebrew term ᶜibrî was applied in the same way to people who moved up into the hills outside of the political and social structures of the city-states.[19]

In his discussion of the Amarna period, Mendenhall seems to deal only with two social categories: the ruling class and the oppressed, the peasants. There is, however, at least one more group mentioned in the Amarna letters, and thus the picture is not as simple as Mendenhall indicates. This group is the ḫupšu (Ugaritic ḫpṯ), "peasant," a class of freeborn citizens who owned small plots of land,[20] and

[15] Cf. Weippert, *The Settlement of the Israelite Tribes in Palestine*, 71ff.

[16] Greenberg, *The Ḫab/piru*, 76. Cf. Gibson, "Some Important Ethnic Terms in the Pentateuch," 234ff.; Halligan, "The Role of the Peasant in the Amarna Period," 21.

[17] See, for instance, Artzi, "'Vox populi' in the el-Amarna Tablets"; W. Helck, "Die Bedrohung Palästinas durch einwandernde Gruppen am Ende der 18. und am Anfang der 19. Dynastie," VT 18 (1968) 472ff.; Koch, "Die Hebräer vom Auszug aus Ägypten," 37ff.; C. H. J. de Geus, *The Tribes of Israel* (Assen and Amsterdam, 1976) 184.

[18] Liverani sees the terms ḫabiru and ᶜibrî as being virtually identical in content, referring to people who have changed, "transgressed," geographically or socially (Hebrew ᶜbr, 'pass over') ("Il fuoruscitismo in Siria nella Tarda età del Bronzo," *Rivista Storia Italiana* 77 [1965] 315–36; and "Farsi Ḫabiru," *Vicino Oriente* 2 [1979] 65–77). Cf. also N. P. Lemche, "'Hebrew' as a National Name for Israel," StTh 33 (1979) 37ff.

[19] One should note that Y. Aharoni (*Land of the Bible*, 176) considers the Amarna ᶜapīru to be Hebrews!

[20] See I. Mendelsohn, "The Canaanite Term for 'Free Proletarian,'" BASOR 83 (1941) 36–39; J. Pedersen, "Note on Hebrew ḥofšī," JPOS (1926) 103ff.; M. Liverani, *Three Amarna Essays* (Malibu, CA, 1979) 17; N. P. Lemche, "The Hebrew Slave," VT 25 (1975) 139ff.; E. Lipiński, "L'esclave

presumably formed the majority of the population in the countryside. The ḫupšu are mentioned in some of the letters of Rib-Adda of Byblos. In EA 81:9–13 he reports that after being encouraged by Abdi-Ashirta of Amurru, some of his people, together with the whole city of Ammia, joined the ʿapīru. In EA 77:36f. he names the ḫupšu as life-threatening agents. In EA 118:21–39, Rib-Adda states that he thinks that the ḫupšu will desert him (not rebel against him). He claims that if they do, the ʿapīru will take over the city. In EA 130:42, on the other hand, Rib-Adda fears that the ḫupšu will rebel against him because there are no provisions to distribute. From these statements, we conclude that ḫupšu and ʿapīru are not identical terms, but that under certain circumstances, the ḫupšu could be classified as ʿapīru. We also see that the letters from Rib-Adda, dating from the 14th century, cannot serve as indications for a peasant revolt in Palestine during the 13th to 12th centuries B.C.

The Tell el-Amarna letters also provide important information for our discussion in their reference to the ʿapīru who were living in the Shechem area and with whom the ruler of Shechem, Labayu, was associated (EA 289:24). If ʿapīru refers in this instance to settled people, perhaps the term could be connected with the Hebrews (i.e., Israelites) in the Shechem area who are mentioned in the biblical texts.[21] The traditions about Jacob and his sons are especially pertinent. The Jacobites are reported to have settled in the areas around or close to Shechem. It is not known how long they had lived there, but the tradition in Gen 32:23–30 of Jacob's name change may reflect an old tradition which remembered that a former transjordanian clan moved into Cisjordan and settled in a territory called Israel.[22] Eventually, they melded together with the local people and became Israelites. How

---

hébreu," *VT* 26 (1976) 120–24. W. von Soden translates, "Angehöriger einer niederen Klasse" (*Akkadisches Handwörterbuch* [Wiesbaden, 1962] 357).

[21] The biblical narrative about Abimelech and Shechem (Judges 9) mirrors the political situation of the Late Bronze period.

[22] Cf. my article, "Some Comments on John Bright's 'History of Israel,'" *JAOS* 95 (1975) 236ff., and O. Eissfeldt, "Jakobs Begegnung mit El und Moses Begegnung mit Jahwe," *OLZ* 58 (1963) col. 331.

large a population lived in the Israelite territory prior to the arrival of the Jacobites is not known. It is also not crucial to decide whether the Jacobite clan was nomadic or sedentary prior to its move to Cisjordan. Biblical tradition seems to have preserved a memory of Jacob's being a "wandering Aramean" (Deut 26:5), and this suggests that the Jacobites were considered by later Israelites to have been nomads originally.[23]

Whether or not Jacob became used as a place-name in the territory of Israel,[24] the name survived because of the clan's assimilation to or association with the highland peoples (i.e., Israel). Because of this, the name Jacob could have been used for a subdivision of the hills. Later on it became a parallel, ideological name for the northern nation, Israel.[25]

The biblical stories of the Gileadite Jephthah and the Bethlehemite David, both of whom became fugitives for a period of their lives, may correspond to the unrest and ʿapīru activities found in the Amarna Letters. Jephthah fled to Tob, a district somewhere beyond Gilead, where he gathered a

[23] I. M. Diakonoff maintains that the term ʾărammi originally meant simply 'nomad' without reference to the language of the tribe" ("Father Adam," *AfO* Beiheft 19 [1982] 19f.). He also refers to "Western Semitic shepherd tribes" and the Hebrews as "being descendants of Šutu or Šitu" (biblical Seth) (p. 19). For the Šutu's probable Aramaic nature, see J. A. Brinkman, *A Political History of Post-Kassite Babylonia 1158–722 B.C.* (Analecta Orientalia 43; Rome, 1968) 280, 285–87.

[24] The name y-ʿ-q-b-r (Jacob-el) occurs in the list of conquered cities in Syria-Palestine of Thutmosis III, but appears from the surrounding names to have been located in Transjordan, perhaps west of Gadara. See Helck, *Die Beziehungen*, 128 and S. Yeivin, "Yaʿqobʾel," *JEA* 45 (1959) 16–18. The same place-name occurs in a list of Ramses II in the temple of Amon at Karnak, but its location is not clear. Helck (*Die Beziehungen*, 210) suggests it may have been in the Eleutheros Valley. For the text, see Simons, *Handbook*, 157, no. 9.

[25] A. Lemaire locates the incoming group, bʿnē yaʿăqôb, in the area northeast of Shechem ("Les Benê Jacob," *RB* 85 [1978] 321ff., 333). He thinks that they were Arameans moving from Haran to Canaan in the 13th century B.C., and that after their arrival, they became associated with a group, "benê Israel," which had left Egypt during the reign of Ramses II ("La Haute Mésopotamie et l'origine des Benê Jacob," *VT* 34 [1984] 95–101).

group of men around himself. He obviously became a successful warrior because the men of Gilead called him home again, offering to make him their ruler. Accepting the position, he was successful in eliminating Ammonite expansion into his land (Judges 11).[26] We should note that the Jephthah story has nothing to do with the peoples of Cisjordan. Jephthah clearly is involved in a transjordanian conflict between Gilead and Ammon, which the biblical narrator has expanded into an "all-Israelite" conflict.[27]

David's activities in the southern hills and his "vassalship" to Achish of Gath can also be compared with those of an ῾apīru leader gathering together a group of young men, perhaps discontents and outcasts, seeking adventure and fortune. The Aramean leader Rezon may be another example of a ῾apīru leader. He established himself against Hadadezer with a band of marauders and others, and eventually was able to settle in Damascus and create a kingdom there (1 Kgs 11:23).[28]

As mentioned in the introduction, archaeological surveys confirm that there was an increase in settlements in the otherwise sparsely populated hills in the 13th–12th centuries B.C. I have maintained elsewhere[29] that the move to the hills could have been due to the desire to escape the wars and upheavals of this period. From the Amarna letters, the only available literary evidence, it is possible to deduce that social unrest and discontent were primary forces which

[26] Jephthah has sometimes been compared with Idrimi of Alalakh. See J. Bright, *A History of Israel* (3rd ed., Philadelphia, 1981) 181. Cf. also Chaney, "Ancient Palestinian Peasant Movements," 83.

[27] The references to the Moabites in this story suggest that the biblical narrator has mixed together different events, showing that the historical memory of these happenings was blurred somewhat.

[28] How much of actual history these three examples relate cannot be known. As M. Liverani ("Memorandum on the Approach to Historiographic Texts," *Orientalia* 42 [1973] 182f.) has mentioned, the Idrimi inscription gives a fairy-tale pattern about the youngest son who rose to power and/or usurped the throne (cf. Hattusili III, Jephthah, David, and the boy king Joash).

[29] Ahlström, "Another Moses Tradition," 65ff.

prompted movement of population groups from all directions. Even though these demographic shifts date from the
previous centuries, the conditions and situations that they
describe are not unique to their moment in history, but can
be found in many times and places. A peasant revolution, on
the other hand, cannot be supported by these letters.[30]

The hill country was a suitable place to go to avoid wars,
the devastation of property, and the tax burdens of the
Egyptians and the city rulers.[31] Due to its difficult terrain,
the hills were seldom penetrated by foreign armies. An
accurate label for the new settlers of the hills would be
"pioneers." The lack of any specific "Israelite" (meaning non-
Canaanite) material culture at the excavated sites in the hills
from the 12th century B.C. may be due to the lack of
expertise and knowledge of advanced techniques practiced
by specialists who remained in the urban centers. As time
passed, the population naturally increased and so also,
perhaps, the cultural achievements.

As a result of the increase of population in the hills, the
agricultural productivity of the land needed to be improved.
While the valleys could yield some crops, some deforestation
and terracing of the slopes were required to increase the
total agricultural yield.[32] An increase in population naturally

[30] The statement in EA 292:28–29 of Baᶜlū-šipti of Gezer that "there
is hostility in the mountains towards me" does not necessarily indicate
that there was a rebellion against him. The statement may merely reflect
the age-old hostility and suspicion between urban and mountain peoples.
The same hostility can be found in Judges 5. Consult Braudel, *The
Mediterranean and the Mediterranean World in the Age of Philip II* 1. 34f.

[31] In addition to the "Canaanites" from the lowland and coastal areas,
other peoples such as Hittites and Jebusites probably settled in the hills.
B. Mazar assumes that they "reached the hill country of Canaan . . . from
the Hittite provinces in Syria and Anatolia at the time of the catastrophe
that overtook the Hittite empire" ("The Early Israelite Settlement in the
Hill Country," *BASOR* 241 [1981] 79).

[32] For terracing, see among others, N. N. Lewis, "Lebanon: The
Mountain and its Terraces," *The Geographical Review* 43 (1953) 1ff.; Z. Ron,
"Agricultural Terraces in the Judean Mountains," *IEJ* 16 (1966) 33ff.;
C. H. J. de Geus, "The Importance of Archaeological Research into the
Palestinian Agricultural Terraces with an Excursus on the Hebrew Word

led to an increase in the size of clans and villages, and the amount of the surrounding land under the cultivation. Conflicts between expanding people in neighboring areas would inevitably have occurred. Smaller clans may have affiliated with larger and more aggressive ones. When conflicts occurred between large clans with the same expansionistic interests in a common territory, war probably would have resulted. This situation in turn would have demanded a more organized society, with rulers capable of steering the communities and organizing their defenses. Aggressive clans and rulers may have been able to increase their territory[33] and their power in this way, resulting eventually in the formation of an extensive political unit, the territorial state.[34]

Gottwald's characterization of the formation of the highland communities as a "retribalization" is misleading.[35] It tends to suggest that the social structures which were used in the villages and settlements were derived from a nomadic or transhumant lifestyle, even though Gottwald believes that most of the new settlements were built by people leaving the urban areas in the coastal and lowland areas. The village organization probably was the same as that used in the villages left behind which had been controlled by the city-states, except that the former overlying royal structure was rejected. Thus, they removed bureaucratic officials and the accompanying taxes and corvée requirements and left the elders as the main governing body, and family-style law

---

gbī," PEQ 107 (1975) 65ff.; and L. E. Stager, "Agriculture," *IDB* Suppl. Vol. (Nashville, 1976) 13. Terracing may have occurred in the hills before 1200 B.C., but after this date it became a widespread practice.

[33] See, for instance, the different theories in H. T. Wright, "Toward an Explanation of the Origin of the State," in *Origins of the State* (ed. R. Cohen and E. R. Service; Philadelphia, 1978) 49ff.

[34] Cf. R. Cohen, who theorizes that "increased centralization of governmental institutions arises out of competition between groups. Populations, or segments of them, vie for access to scarce resources, and ultimately this process leaves one group dominant, at least for a time" ("Introduction" in *Origins of the State* [ed. R. Cohen and E. R. Service; Philadelphia, 1978] 6).

[35] Gottwald, *The Tribes of Yahweh*, 323ff.

and custom as the forces regulating social behavior. As the villages grew, further hierarchical structuring may have emerged. They may have added a leading elder, chieftain, or ruler to make final decisions and to head the increasingly more complex controlling organ which was developing to regulate life and to balance opposing groups and interests in a workable system.[36] Thus, social differentiation would lead to a centralization of the power structure and, at the same time, to the emergence of an administrative apparatus.[37] When a pioneer group therefore had grown and expanded its land holdings, its political organization would likewise have become more complex, and eventually it would evolve into the same type of system used in the city-states that they had left.[38]

Sociologically, the new hill settlements could be characterized by the Hebrew term *bêt ʾāb*, 'father's house,' or the plural form *bêt ʾābôt*. This term could be used more loosely to refer to an extended family,[39] i.e., the descendants and their families (cf. Gen 12:1ff.; Num 3:24, 34:14, etc.). In the latter passage *bêt ʾāb* is clearly a term for a larger family group within a clan, a *mišpāḥâh*. It is impossible to know whether several *bêt ʾābôt* in the same village were related or not. Originally, a village may have been inhabited by unrelated families.[40] As time passed, people probably intermarried,

---

[36] Cf. L. Krader, *Dialectic of Civil Society* (Assen and Amsterdam, 1976) 11f.

[37] Thus, for instance, C. E. Larsen, *Life and Land Use on the Bahrain Islands: The Geoarchaeology of an Ancient Society* (Chicago, 1983) 105.

[38] This may throw some light on the Israelites' request for a king "as all peoples" (1 Sam 8:5).

[39] Cf. J. Scharbert, "Beyt ʾAb als sociologische Grösse im Alten Testament," in *Von Kanaan bis Kerala* (Festschrift J. P. M. van der Ploeg; AOAT 211; ed. W. C. Delsman et al.; Neukirchen-Vluyn, 1982) 213–37. See also de Geus, *The Tribes of Israel*, 127ff., 134ff.; J. Sapin, "La géographie humaine de la Syrie-Palestine au deuxième millénaire avant J.-C. voie de recherche historique," *JESHO* 25 (1982) 37f.

[40] G. E. Mendenhall, "Social Organization in Early Israel," in *Magnalia Dei* (ed. F. M. Cross et al.; Garden City, NY, 1976) 143ff. N. K. Gottwald sees the *mišpāḥâh* as representing the neighborhood rather than being a term for a family or clan (*The Tribes of Yahweh*, 316f.).

which would have extended, or rather expanded, the clan. The practice of clustering houses wall to wall, thereby creating a *ḥāṣēr*, 'court,'[41] may have been based on geographical or protective considerations as much as on family relationships. Therefore, this practice cannot be used to argue that bedouins settled at a given place. Some of the earliest Iron Age I settlements in the hills and the Negev may have been founded by one or two related or unrelated families. Tel Masos would be an illustration of a *ḥāṣēr*-type settlement with houses built wall to wall. Raddana[42] and Giloh, both in the hills, may be seen as examples of extended *bêt ʾāb* settlements.[43] The excavations have not yet given any indication as to whether these latter two settlements were of the *ḥāṣēr*-type.

The *ḥāṣēr*-type settlement is not a new development in the Early Iron Age. In the Negev highlands and the southern Sinai, a settlement has been found which is "an amalgamation of the long-familiar sunken broadroom with the emerging concept of a central courtyard: it was this model that came to characterize the EB II culture of these desert regions."[44] The phenomenon, however, is much older than that. Semi-circular and circular houses or living quarters with a central courtyard surrounded by small rooms have, for instance, been found at Tell Murēybit in northern Syria dating from ca. 5500 B.C.[45]

---

[41] Cf. A. Kempinski, D. Zichmoni, E. Gilboa, N. Rösel, "Excavations at Tel Masos 1972, 1974, 1975," *Eretz Israel* 15 (1981) 177, fig. 12. For placenames reflecting this, cf. Hazeroth, Hazor, Hazar-Shual.

[42] See J. A. Callaway and R. E. Cooley, "A Salvage Excavation at Raddana, in Bireh," *BASOR* 210 (1971) 9ff.

[43] We are not concerned at present with trying to determine the population in the hills or the number of people who could live in one house. For the latter issue, see R. Naroll, "Floor Area and Settlement Population," *American Antiquity* 27 (1962) 587–89; and R. M. Adams, *Heartland and Cities* (Chicago, 1981). Adams estimates that there were 3.5 persons per family in ancient Palestine (p. 144).

[44] I. Beit-Arieh, "A Pattern of Settlement in Southern Sinai and Southern Canaan in the Third Millennium B.C.," *BASOR* 243 (1981) 51.

[45] O. Aurenche, *La maison orientale: L'architecture du proche orient ancien des origines au milieu du quartrième millénaire*, I: *Texte* (Bibliothèque Français Archéologiques et Historique 109; Paris, 1981) 188.

Alongside clan membership, geographical proximity was an important factor which created solidarity between people. "Kinship and locality serve everywhere to link people together."[46] The influence of geography is exemplified by Solomon's district division. Areas which formed natural geographical units were part of the same districts. District 2, for instance, included Timnah, Beth-Shemesh, Ono, Lod, Aphek, which were geographically contiguous. District 5 comprised valley regions and stretched from Megiddo down to Adam in the Jordan Valley and included the cities of Taanach, Ibleam, Dothan, and Beth Shan.[47] This probably reflects a process of tribalization in which peoples and clans of the same geographical area had banded together previously and organized community affairs, labor, and defense.

Our reconstruction of the settlement of the central Palestinian hills and the emergence of the Israelite monarchy may be aided by some observations which L. Marfoe has made in his investigation of sociopolitical and settlement problems in southern Syria.[48] In particular, the parallels he cites from the later Arab period might be useful in helping us understand that the hostility and suspicion of mountain people toward lowland people is a long-standing tradition. His theory that smaller groups that take refuge in a new territory often convert to the religion of the new "home" may also be useful, although the hills in Palestine were so sparsely settled at the end of the LB II period that many of the new settlements were built on virgin soil. In this case, one cannot talk about "conversion," since the few settled areas would probably have had the same religion as the rest of Canaan.[49] While we may suppose that there were local

[46] I. Schapera, *Government and Politics in Tribal Societies* (New York, 1956) 4.

[47] Cf. my *Royal Administration and National Religion in Ancient Palestine*, 33f.

[48] L. Marfoe, "The Integrative Transformation: Patterns of Sociopolitical Organization in Southern Syria," *BASOR* 234 (1979) 32ff.

[49] The "plaque-figurines" of the Late Bronze period have been found in early Iron Age strata in the hill country, and they continue into Iron II in some sites in the northern kingdom of Israel. In Judah, on the other hand, these figurines "are generally absent from Iron II sites" (M. Tadmor, "Female Cult Figurines in Late Canaan and Early Israel: Archaeological

differences in the common religious system, it is inappropriate to use the term "conversion" when discussing acceptance of particular local traditions.

As a final observation, Marfoe advocates that the growth of the Israelite kingdom is not only to be understood as a sociopolitical phenomenon, but must also be attributed to the ideological uniqueness of Israel's monarchy.[50] How do we find this uniqueness, though, when the textual material upon which we have to build our reconstruciton reflects the theological and factional views of a later time? And how unique was the Israelite monarchy when the only kingship model available to Saul and David was the surrounding Syro-Palestinian one?[51]

Evidence," *SPDS,* 172). This shows that no change occurred in the religion in the hills in the early Iron I period.

[50] He maintains that "since it is the theory and practice of the Israelite ideology that is the most prominent feature of the monarchy, a failure to understand these ties would in essence be a failure to understand the monarchy itself (Marfoe, "The Integrative Transformation," 34).

[51] Of course, there were some variations in this rulership pattern. In the Amarna Age, for instance, Abdi-Ashirta of Amurru was never given the title "king" or "prince" in the correspondence, and we do not know of any capital of Amurru. M. Liverani (*Three Amarna Essays,* 15) thinks the reigning house of Abdi-Ashirta consisted of "a family of chiefs recognized as such by various local groups of pastoralists." Could not the same be said for some of the judges of the pre-monarchic period? Other forms of government were known, though, namely that of the foreigners, the Philistines and possibly also the Gibeonites. How different they were from the normal Canaanite kingship system is not known. We know that the Philistine rulers had the title *seren,* which could be cognate to the Hittite *tarwanaš,* 'judge,' and Greek *týrannos,* 'tyrant.' See M. Riemschneider, "Die Herkunft der Philister," *Acta Antiqua* 4 (1956) 17f., and W. Helck, who mentions that Luwian princes were called *tar-wa-na-s* ("Ein sprachliches Indiz für die Herkunft der Philister," *Biblische Notizen* 21 [1983] 31, and cf. T. C. Mitchel, "Philistia," in *Archaeology and Old Testament Study* [ed. D. W. Thomas; Oxford, 1967] 413). We learn that at a later time the Philistine population of the city of Ekron was divided into three categories: 1) the *šakkanakkē* = the military chiefs; 2) the *rubē* = the nobility; 3) the *nišē* = the people (also called *mārē alē,* 'the sons of the cities') (D. D. Luckenbill, *Annals of Senacherib* [OIP 2], II:73, III:8). As to the Gibeonite city-league we have no information as to how it was governed. The text in Josh 9:11 mentions their elders but it is not clear whether this was part of their original system or a later adaptation.

3

Some Evidence from Archaelogy

The beginning of the so-called "Iron Age" is usually dated to
ca. 1200 B.C. This does not mean, however, that iron became
the most common raw material for tools and objects. The
designation "Iron Age" is part of a comfortable periodization,
which justifies the name because of the first appearance of
objects made from iron. We must not imagine that the new
techniques for making iron tools contributed to an increase
in the population of the central hills of Palestine. Were this
the case, the excavations should have yielded a sharp increase in iron tools and iron objects from that time. But such
is not the case. Iron production and use spread slowly. There
is some increase in iron objects, such as agricultural tools,
after 1200, but iron did not replace bronze at that time.[1]
This means that iron implements cannot be used as an
indication for an increase in population in the hills around
1200 B.C.

Archaeological surveys, on the other hand, provide firm
evidence that the population in the hill country increased at
this time. In the so-called "Manasseh-Ephraim-Benjamin
territories" (to use the biblical terms) there was an increase
in settlement sites from about 50 in the LB II period to ca.
115 in the Early Iron I period.[2] In the Shechem area alone 14

[1] Jane C. Waldbaum, "The First Archaeological Appearance of Iron and
the Transition to the Iron Age," in *The Coming of the Age of Iron* (ed. T. A.
Wertime and J. D. Muhly; New Haven and London, 1980) 86.
[2] See M. Kochavi et al., *Judea, Samaria, and the Golan: Archaeological Survey
1967–68* (Hebrew; Jerusalem, 1972); E. F. Campbell, "The Shechem Area
Survey," *BASOR* 190 (1968) 19ff., 40ff.

sites turned up pottery of the LB II–Early Iron I phase showing that there was no significant break in the pottery tradition. This survey also showed that during the MB II period Shechem "was a virtually isolated impregnable city with hardly any surrounding villages." The first increase in settlements was around 1450 B.C.[3] In contrast to the central hills, archaeological work in the area around Hebron has indicated that this region had almost no population during the LB II period. According to Kochavi's survey, the sites in Judah go down from four in the LB II period to three in the Early Iron I period.[4] Therefore, most of the Judean hills were probably a no-man's land.

Changes in material culture usually have been explained as a result of new peoples moving into the country. However, this explanation is too simplistic to solve an intricate problem. It does not take into consideration the needs of a growing society or community, nor the development of technical skills such as tools, nor the organization of public works.[5] Neither does it consider the possibility that one and the same potter could have developed new pottery forms and variant rim styles.

The material culture of the hill country during the 13th–12th centuries B.C. does not support the theory that a new semi-nomadic people occupied the whole mountainous region of Palestine. Nor does it indicate that substantial changes in the material culture occurred.[6] Because new settlements were often built on previously unsettled sites, the builders could not have borrowed their technical knowledge from previous inhabitants, as has been suggested, for instance, by Y. Aharoni.[7]

[3] Campbell, "The Shechem Area Survey," 40. For a chart of settlement variations, see Marfoe, "The Integrative Transformation," 31.

[4] P. C. Hammond, "Hebron," *RB* 72 (1965) 267ff.; Kochavi et al., *Judea, Samaria, and the Golan*, 20, 83. Cf. also T. L. Thompson, *The Settlement of Palestine in the Bronze Age* (Tübinger Atlas des Vorderen Orients: Riehe B, Geisteswiss., 34; Wiesbaden, 1979) 48–50.

[5] Cf. the criticism by Chaney, "Ancient Palestinian Peasant Movements," 46.

[6] Cf. H. J. Franken, "Palestine During the Nineteenth Dynasty. (1b) Archaeological Evidence," *CAH*[3] II/2 (Cambridge, 1975) 331ff.

[7] *The Land of the Bible*, 240.

J. A. Callaway has concluded from the archaeological remains at Ai that the new settlers in this area were "primarily farmers." They came "from a background of agricultural life, either in the hill country elsewhere, or in the lowlands among hills."[8] He thinks that the people originated "in the lowland region west of the hill country. Settlement of the coastal region by maritime peoples may have pressured the villagers to move inland."[9] The settlements in the area of Ai are usually unwalled, with pier-constructed houses (known elsewhere in Palestine in the area west of the hilly regions),[10] cisterns, and cobbled streets. Their founders also terraced the hillsides to increase the amount of land available for food production. It is clear from their building tradition and agricultural expertise that these people were not nomadic or semi-nomadic.[11]

The origin of at least some of the hill settlers in the lowland area may also be supported by the building remains at Khirbet Raddana. Like the Ai houses, they seem to indicate a connection with the building tradition of the coastal area.[12] Raddana's settlers can be seen to belong to an early wave of people moving up to the hills in the 14th century, as Y. Aharoni has already pointed out.[13]

The material culture of the central hill country of the 14th–13th centuries B.C. was mainly Canaanite, as was that

[8] J. A. Callaway, "Excavating Ai (et-Tell): 1964–1972," *BA* 39 (1976) 29f.; cf. J. A. Graham, *The Third Campaign at Tell el-Ful: The Excavations of 1964* (ed. Nancy Lapp; AASOR 45; Cambridge, MA, 1981) 35.

[9] Callaway, "Excavating Ai (et-Tell)," 29.

[10] See my article, "The Early Iron Age Settlers at Tēl Masos (Ḥirbet el-Mšāš)," *ZDPV* 100 (1984), 35–52.

[11] et-Tell is the only hill settlement which has evidence of a possible disturbance and change in population. Callaway ("Excavating Ai [et-Tell]," 30) maintains that around 1150–1125 B.C. a new population moved into the area near Ai and Raddana, based on the destruction of the cobbled streets, the expansion of houses to accommodate more people, and the building of silos above ground. Since the pottery tradition remained Canaanite, however, it should not be concluded that the new group was invading Israelites.

[12] Cf. L. E. Stager, "The Archaeology of the Family in Ancient Israel," *BASOR* 258 (1985) 2ff., 11f.

[13] Y. Aharoni, "Khirbet Raddana and its Inscriptions," *IEJ* 21 (1971) 135.

of the new settlements in the Negev dating from ca. 1200
B.C. and later. This is evident from the house styles and
pottery forms. The type of house found at different places in
these areas is the same type used in the regions west of the
hills.[14] As to pottery, so-called "biblical archaeologists" have
had a hard time finding anything typically Israelite, that is,
new and different, in the material culture of 12th century
sites. However, as soon as someone has detected a pot with a
slightly different form or a variant pot rim, it has been
labeled as Israelite. The best-known example of this is the
so-called "collared rim jar." When it was first uncovered, it
was pronounced to be an Israelite type unknown in Canaan
before ca. 1200 B.C. Examples from Hazor (14th century)[15]
and other places were shown to be Canaanite forms with
antecedents in the LB II tradition.[16] We should also note that
the main pottery tradition of the Late Bronze period continued into the Iron Age.[17] This continuity has been illus-
trated in a tomb at Dothan in which there is no break in
pottery styles from LB II to the Iron I period. Both periods
are represented in the same level (level 2) in the cave.[18]

The following brief review of recently excavated sites in
the hills will demonstrate the untenability of an "invasion"
hypothesis. Giloh, southwest of Jerusalem, appears to have
been settled around 1200 B.C. The excavator, A. Mazar, has
assumed that the settlers were incoming Israelites of the

---

[14] Cf. my discussion in *JNES* 39 (1980) 65ff., and my article, "The Early
Iron Age Settlers at Ṭel-Māśōś (Ḥirbet el-Mšāš)."

[15] Y. Yadin et al., *Hazor III–IV* (Jerusalem, 1961) pl. 275:11, 12.

[16] See, for instance, H. Franken, "The Problem of Identification in
Biblical Archaeology," *PEQ* 108 (1976) 8. Consult also M. M. Ibrahim,
"The Collared Rim Jar of the Early Iron Age," in *Archaeology in the Levant*
(Essays for Kathleen M. Kenyon) (ed. R. Moorey and P. Parr; Warminster,
1978) 116–26; W. Rast, *Taanach I: Studies in the Iron Age Pottery* (ASOR
Excavation Reports; Cambridge, MA, 1978) 9.

[17] Cf. Amiran, *Ancient Pottery of the Holy Land*, 191.

[18] J. P. Free, "The Seventh Season at Dothan," *BASOR* 160 (1960) 6ff.
Cf. E. F. Campbell, "Two Amarna Notes: The Shechem City-State and
Amarna Administrative Terminology," in *Magnalia Dei* (ed. F. M. Cross
et al.; New York, 1976) 44.

tribe of Judah.[19] This view has two weaknesses: in addition to its unquestioning acceptance of the settlers' identity as newly-arrived Israelites, it also assumes that the tribe of Judah was a functioning unit at that time, even though we do not know anything about a tribe of Judah as a historical fact until the time of David.[20] With this in mind, the archaeological remains from Giloh cannot be used to prove that newly-arrived Judahites infiltrated the area around Jerusalem. The site's material culture is described as mainly Canaanite.[21] The logical conclusion, then, is that a group of Canaanites had settled at Giloh. Another possibility would

[19] A. Mazar, "Giloh: An Early Israelite Settlement near Jerusalem," *IEJ* 31 (1981) 1–36.

[20] Judah's origin is somewhat obscure. The Bible indicates that the "tribe" was made up of several different clans, of which many originally were Edomites. See also the discussion in chap. 4.

[21] As examples of pottery found at Giloh, Mazar mentions "a rim fragment of a chalice also found at Tell Qasîle Stratum XII" (p. 20), which was Philistine. Other parallels to Qasîle (stratum XII) include some disc bases which "are typical of the LB, but also continue during the twelfth century" (p. 20). The bowls of the 'beveled' rim type "started to appear in the LB and continued in use in some Early Iron Age I contexts." This type of pottery "does not appear in sites like Tell en-Naṣbeh, ʿAi and the Iron Age I strata in Bethel" (p. 21). The collared rim pithos is a type mainly occurring at Megiddo, Taʿanak, ʿAfula and the coastal area (Tel Mevorakh, Tel Zeror, Tell Qasîle, Aphek and ʿIzbet Ṣarṭah), in the central hills (Shiloh, Bethel, ʿAi, Raddana, Tell el-Fûl), and in Beth Shemesh, Tell Beit Mirsim, and Beth Zur, the last two being the southern border of this type. It is rare in the Shepelah (pp. 27ff.). This type is also found in Sahab in Transjordan, a site not considered as Israelite by Mazar (p. 30). The storage jar examples (two) found at Giloh ("oval body, sloping shoulders, thickened, everted rim and narrow base") belong to a type occurring mainly in the south of Palestine during the 13th century (pp. 23ff.). "Similar rims and bases can be found in the Iron Age I sites of the central mountains," for example, Shiloh, Tell en-Naṣbeh, Bethel, Beth-Zur (cf. also Gezer and Tel Batash). We should note that one example is also found at Tell Qasîle (stratum XII or XI, according to Mazar). This type is very rare in northern Palestine (p. 25). These examples from such different sites as Megiddo, Tell Qasîle, and Sahab show that we are dealing with Palestinian traditions rather than a pottery tradition of a special ethnic group. Cf. the discussion in Weippert, *The Settlement of the Israelite Tribes in Palestine*, 133f.; and Ibrahim, "The Collared Rim Jar of the Early Iron Age," 116–26.

be that the site was built by Jerusalemites as a Jebusite outpost. At this time, it is not known whether the material culture of Jerusalem was different from that which is commonly termed Canaanite. Since Jerusalem had existed for several centuries prior to 1200, one may assume that its material culture probably was an extension of the culture of the land. The abandonment of Giloh around 1000 B.C. is probably related to a water storage problem since no cisterns or wells have been found there. Had Judahites conquered the area and built the site, it is unlikely that they would have given up a place so close to Jerusalem, since Jerusalem was a major goal in their alleged conquest plans.

The finds from Tell Jedur near Hebron[22] also contradict the hypothesis that all new settlements in the Judean hills founded during the 13th–12th centuries B.C. would have been built by invading Israelites who were a distinctive ethnic group with a "non-Canaanite" culture. The remains from this site reflect the culture of Canaan at this time. Among the finds, for instance, was a burial cave containing some metal objects, pottery, alabaster vases, and weapons. The pottery consisted mainly of local ware, but included also Cypriot and Aegean types.[23] There was also a so-called "Midianite" style bowl. These objects range in date from the 14th century to the end of the 13th century. Thus, Tell Jedur does not indicate that a new people moved into the area at the end of the LB II period, which is the time frame in which A. Mazar places the settlement of the "tribe of Judah" in these parts of the country.[24]

The recent excavations at Tell Marjamme (co-ord. 155–182, 13 km. northeast of Beitin at Wādī Siᶜah opposite Dahr Mirzabâneh) have not yet shown "any traces of permanent settlement" for the LB II–Early Iron I period. As far as has

[22] S. Ben-Arieh, "Tell Jedur," *Eretz Israel* 15 (1981) 115–28 (= 81*).

[23] V. Hankey, "The Aegean Pottery of Khirbet Judur," *Eretz Israel* 15 (1981) 32*–38*. It is interesting to note that some freshwater mussels were also found at Tell Jedur, see H. K. Mienis, "African Freshwater Mussels from a Late Bronze Tomb at Jdur: Har Hebron," *Eretz Israel* 15 (1981) 128.

[24] Mazar, "Giloh: An Early Israelite Settlement Near Jerusalem," 1–26.

been established there was a large unwalled settlement at the site during the LB I period through the 14th century B.C. For the following time there is some pottery from Late Bronze II–Iron I but a permanent settlement has not yet been found. Thus, no newcomers seem to have settled at this place in the Early Iron I period.[25] From the time of the United Monarchy, a large, fortified city (ca. 10 acres) occupied the site.[26]

ᶜIzbet Ṣarṭah, ca. 3 km. east of Aphek, has also been labeled Israelite. It was settled during the 13th–11th centuries B.C. Very little has been reported from the site. Among the few finds mentioned by the excavators are a "Mycenaean pyxis, a krater fragment of the 'Ibex and Palm-tree' type" and another fragment with the same motif. Also, a so-called "four-room house" was found. The site was abandoned in the beginning of the 10th century B.C. (at the latest) but the reason is not known.[27] If the population was Philistine, presumably the change of rulership over this area with the expansion of David's kingdom caused the Philistines to move.

One of the main criteria used to defend an Israelite origin is an ostracon, sometimes characterized as an abecedary, which was recovered from the site.[28] M. Kochavi and

[25] M. Zohar, "Tell Marjammah (ᶜEin Sâmiyeh)," *IEJ* 30 (1980) 219ff.

[26] A. Mazar, "Three Israelite Sites in the Hills of Judah and Ephraim," *BA* 45 (1982) 171ff.

[27] M. Kochavi and I. Finkelstein, "ᶜIzbet Ṣarṭah," *IEJ* 28 (1978) 267f. The recent investigations by I. Finkelstein show 67 new sites in the hills east of ᶜIzbet Ṣarṭah for which no Late Bronze settlements could be found. 12 of them showed Early Bronze remains and nine Middle Bronze remains. The investigation covered an area of ca. 40 by 35 km. with Upper Beth Horon in the south and Kh. Sh. Nasrallah in the north ("The ᶜIzbet Ṣarṭah Excavations and the Israelite Settlement in the Hill Country" (unpub. Ph.D. diss.; Tel Aviv, 1983). (I am indebted to Mrs. Diana Edelman for this information.) The origin of these new settlers is disputed. Many probably came from the lowlands. Some could have been ᶜapīru settling down (cf. the discussion above) and as peoples settling in the territory Israel, they all could have been known as Israelites.

[28] See M. Kochavi, "An Ostracon of the Period of the Judges from ᶜIzbet Ṣarṭah, *Tel Aviv* 4 (1977) 1ff.; A. Dotan, "New Light on the ᶜIzbet Ṣarṭah Ostracon," *Tel Aviv* 8 (1981) 170ff. Other Early Iron I sites found in

A. Demsky have concluded that its script is Hebrew.[29] Since it has not yet been demonstrated convincingly that an Israelite conquest actually occurred, and since we know that the predominant culture of the land at this time was Canaanite, it would make the most sense to classify this writing as Canaanite. This is particularly true when, as A. Dotan has pointed out, the personal names on this ostracon are Canaaneo-Phoenician. This is not surprising since the ostracon comes from the Canaaneo-Phoenician world. Nonetheless, Dotan also sees the script as Hebrew.[30] F. M. Cross is opposed to calling the script Hebrew, maintaining that there is "strong evidence that the alphabet in Israel continued to be the common Old Canaanite script until its evolution into Early Linear Phoenician and indeed shared the Early Linear Phoenician with chancelleries of Phoenicia into the 10th century."[31]

The whole discussion of a Hebrew-Israelite vs. Phoenicio-Canaanite script is meaningless because it rests on the faulty assumption that Israelites took over the country shortly before 1200 B.C. As should be clear from the current

---

the Sharon plain and in the foothills of the central mountains also have been labeled "Israelite" by M. Garsiel and I. Finkelstein ("The Westward Expansion of the House of Joseph in the Light of ⁽Izbet Ṣarṭah Excavations," *Tel Aviv* 5 [1978] 192–98.

[29] M. Kochavi and A. Demsky, "A Proto-Canaanite Abecedary dating from the Period of the Judges and its Implications for the History of the Alphabet," *Tel Aviv* 4 (1977) 20f.

[30] Dotan, "New Light on the ⁽Izbet Ṣarṭah Ostracon," 171. J. Naveh prefers to call the ostracon's script proto-Canaanite ("Some Considerations on the Ostracon from ⁽Izbet Ṣarṭah," *IEJ* 28 [1978] 33). It is, of course, possible that Philistines also have settled at this site and that the ostracon indicates their interest in learning the language of the land (cf. Naveh, "Some Considerations on the Ostracon from ⁽Izbet Ṣarṭah," 35). Naveh also thinks that the inscription has "been scratched by a semi-literate person," (*The Early History of the Alphabet* [Jerusalem and Leiden, 1982] 37).

[31] F. M. Cross, "Newly Found Inscriptions in Old Canaanite and Early Phoenician Scripts," *BASOR* 238 (1980) 13. Cross states that "a Hebrew national script has been proclaimed before it has separated from the Old Canaanite script" (p. 13).

investigation, such an assumption is not supported by archaeological finds. Unfortunately, pottery assemblages and floor plans have not been published yet for ᶜIzbet Ṣarṭah because of the focus on the ostracon, so one cannot use the most reliable criteria to determine the cultural background of this site's settlers. In light of our current knowledge about the history of Canaan, however, it would be better to attribute differences in old Canaanite scripts which date between the 12th and 11th centuries B.C. to local differences or untrained hands rather than to national distinctions. Because the majority of the Israelites were originally Canaanites one cannot expect them to have changed their script when they moved up to the hills. A Hebrew national script could not have come into existence before there was a Hebrew nation with its own administrative centers.

Tel Ṣippor (Tell et-Tuyur), ca. 3 km. northwest of modern Kiryat Gat, is another site which has been associated with the supposed newcomers, the Israelites. This settlement, like Giloh and Tell Jedur, shows a general continuity in material culture from LB II through the Early Iron I period. The pottery assemblage of stratum III (LB II) is typical of the last phase of Late Bronze–beginning Iron I Canaanite ware.[32] This stratum also contains some imported Mycenaean pottery, as well as a stone statuette in Egyptian style of a seated god or king holding a lotus flower in his hand.[33] The statuette indicates the longstanding Egyptian influence on the Canaanite culture. Strata II and I continued to yield predominantly Canaanite pottery but also included Philistine ware. Stratum I ended shortly before 1000 B.C., at which time the site seems to have been abandoned. At the time of the emergence of the united Israelite monarchy then, Tel Ṣippor ceased to exist.[34] From these data, we conclude that Tel Ṣippor was a Canaanite settlement which later could have come under Philistine rule.

[32] A. Biran, "Tel Ṣippor," *EAEHL* IV (Jerusalem, 1978) 1112f.

[33] Biran, "Tel Ṣippor," 1112f.

[34] A. Biran and Ora Negbi, "The Stratigraphical Sequence at Tel Ṣippor," *IEJ* (1966) 160ff.

Archaeology seems to indicate that there was also an increase in settlements in the Negev[35] in the Early Iron Age I period.[36] This increase starts in the 12th century, for instance at Beer-sheba (stratum IX) and Arad (stratum XII), and Tel Masos (stratum III).[37] Something must have happened around 1000 B.C. because one of the sites, Tel Masos, seems to have been abandoned at that time. This phenomenon is perhaps not too astonishing in light of the stories about David who, as a Philistine war lord, marauded in the territory south of the Judean hills, destroying settlements and killing their population (1 Sam 27:8ff.). The reason for people moving into the Negev may have been the same as for the move into the hills: the desire to escape the bad times.[38]

Among the Negev settlements built around 1200 B.C. is Tel Masos (Khirbet el-Meshâsh). The excavators have posited that this site was built by invading semi-nomadic

[35] Cf. also Z. Herzog, "Enclosed Settlements in the Negeb and the Wilderness of Beer-sheba," *BASOR* 250 (1983) 40f. Herzog assumes that the pits of Beer-sheba stratum IX represent an Israelite settlement. Arad stratum XII he sees as Kenite, and Tel Masos as Amalekite (p. 47). For the impossibility of seeing Tel Masos as the city of Amalek, see my article "The Early Iron Age Settlers at Ṭēl Māśōś," 50ff.

[36] In the light of the examples discussed (except Tel Ṣippor), W. G. Dever ("Monumental Architecture in Ancient Israel in the Period of the United Monarchy," *SPDS*, 286) prematurely concludes that these small sites "tend to confirm the view of Alt and Noth on the Israelite occupation of Canaan."

[37] Tel Esdar (between Beer-sheba and Dimona) can also be mentioned. It was not settled between the Early Bronze II and Iron I periods. The houses of stratum III (Iron I) were built close to each other on the top of the mound forming a "walled" village to the outside world. The site was destroyed in the 11th century B.C.; see M. Kochavi, "Tel Esdar," *EAEHL* IV, 1169f.

[38] Herzog has proposed that the increase was a "result of Philistine pressure in the Shephela of Judah that drove the ever-increasing Israelite population into the more arid zones in the south" ("Enclosed Settlements in the Negeb and the Wilderness of Beer-sheba," 47). As I have maintained, however, Judah was not really Israelite during this period of Philistine hegemony.

Israelites who had escaped from Egypt.[39] Among their arguments for an Israelite founding of Tel Masos is the occurrence of the so-called "four-room house," which has been seen as a refinement of the bedouin tent.[40] However, we do not have any information about any form of bedouin tent from the period ca. 1200 B.C. At the same time, the excavators have admitted that the material culture of the site is Canaanite. The logical conclusion to be drawn from the remains, therefore, is that the builders of Tel Masos were indigenous people of Canaan, not invading Israelites. The excavators have based their identity on later religious texts which are intended to tell about the wonders performed by Yahweh in olden times, rather than to communicate firm facts. Tel Masos was one of the Negev sites which was abandoned around 1000 B.C. The reason for this is not known,[41] but David could have been responsible.

In summary, most Palestinian or biblical archaeologists have had a hard time finding anything typically Israelite (i.e., different from Canaanite) in the 12th century material culture of ancient Palestine. Knowing that the archaeological remains of houses found in the hills from the time of the 12th century B.C. are the same types as those in the lowlands and the coastal area, and knowing that the majority of pottery is a continuation of the Late Bronze II Canaanite pottery tradition, the logical conclusion is that much of the population of the hill country was Canaanite. While we have no texts from 1200 which tell us why these people moved up into the hills, it is likely that the unstable political situation around 1200 B.C. was a major contributing factor to the increase in hill country settlements. The few "new" or "different" pot and rim forms which have been distinguished

---

[39] A. Kempinski and V. Fritz, "Excavations at Tel Masos (Khirbet el-Meshâsh): Preliminary Report of the Third Season," *Tel Aviv* 4 (1977) 146ff.

[40] Kempinski and Fritz, "Excavations at Tel Masos," 146ff.

[41] For a fuller discussion of this problem, see my article, "The Early Iron Age Settlers at Ṭēl Māśōś (Ḥirbet el-Mšāš)." I also argue that Masos is not the city of Amalek.

tentatively, or which might be found in future work, can
just as well be seen to be part of an artistic development of
the existing pottery traditions as evidence that a new, non-
Canaanite people had invaded the country. On the other
hand, we should expect to find some genuine non-Canaanite
forms at some sites, since it is likely that groups moved into
the hills from the south, north, and east which were part of
another cultural tradition. We have mentioned, for instance,
that some Edomite groups have relocated in this region, and
Aramaean or Hittite groups may have also.[42] The finds
which have been labeled "poor" do not automatically indicate
the presence of semi-nomads; rather, they indicate that the
peoples moving up to the hills had less expertise and perhaps
fewer raw materials than those who remained in the coastal
and urban areas where industries were more developed.
Furthermore, the use of terracing technology to create
arable land in the hills clearly indicates an agricultural
background.[43] Thus, the new hill settlers could best be
characterized as pioneers.

[42] Generally speaking, the hill country probably has been a suitable
place for refugees at various times. This could have been the case at the
time of the upheavals through which the Ugaritic and Hittite kingdoms
came to an end (cf. B. Mazar, "The Early Israelite Settlement in the Hill
Country," *BASOR* 241 [1981] 79). Peoples may, of course, have come to
the hills in earlier periods. There are, for instance, old connections with
Anatolia and the Amuq valley (S. Hood, "Excavations at Tabara el-Akrad,
1948–49," *Anatolian Studies* 1 [1951] 113–47; cf. R. J. and Linda Braidwood,
Excavations in the Plains of Antioch. I: The Earliest Assemblages, Phases A–J
[Chicago, 1960] 82). The Khirbet Kerak ware is one indication, not only
for trade contacts, but for northerners having settled in Palestine (cf.
D. L. Esse, *Beyond Subsistence: Beth Yerah and Northern Palestine in the Early Bronze
Age* [unpubl. Ph.D. diss., University of Chicago, 1982] 244f., 317ff.).

[43] Cf. my article, "Where Did the Israelites Live?" *JNES* 41 (1982) 133f.

4

The Territory of Israel

In chap. 2, I discussed the biblical tradition about the Jacobite clans, who are depicted as having moved from Transjordan into the Shechem area, where they settled and melded together with the local population, and became Israelites. This suggests that Israel could have been the name of the territory around Shechem. We can now ask whether the area into which the Jacobites moved was the same as that mentioned on the Merneptah stela (from the end of the 13th century B.C.). If so, was it the same geographical district in which the ʿapīru lived who were associated with Labayu's kingdom in the Amarna Age? Can we also associate this area with the place where Samuel reports that Moses and Aaron settled a group who later became known as Israelites (1 Sam 12:8)? (Note that Moses and Aaron are still alive and healthy and leading the people into the hill country in this tradition!)[1]

The Merneptah stela focuses mainly on this pharaoh's Libyan campaign in his fifth year (ca. 1208 B.C.), but the closing section summarizes his Syro-Palestinian campaign. It is here that the name Israel first appears in a non-biblical text. J. A. Spalinger has pointed out that the stela is a specimen of "rhetorical military texts" which gives little

---

[1] Even the deuteronomist was not able to censure this note. Perhaps he was not familiar with the final "retrodating" of the "Exodus-Wanderings-Conquest" narrative. For 1 Sam 12:8, see my article, "Another Moses Tradition," 65ff.

information about actual military events, and that the primary purpose of the closing coda section is to present "the peaceful state of Egypt."[2] Because there is an independent reference to this Syro-Palestinian campaign however, we know that it is not merely literary fiction. The Amada stela[3] characterizes Merneptah as the "Reducer of Gezer," and Gezer is named in the coda section as one of the three city-states which the pharaoh conquered. Thus, while we cannot be completely certain about the extent of Merneptah's campaign from the description in the coda, which, except for the city-states, uses common terms and names associated with Syria-Palestine in general,[4] we can conclude that he mounted a campaign in Palestine,[5] and took at least the three city-states listed (Ashkelon, Gezer, and Yenoᶜam) and probably encountered a group called Israel.[6]

[2] J. A. Spalinger, *Aspects of the Military Documents of the Ancient Egyptians* (Yale Near Eastern Researches 9; New Haven and London, 1982) 239, 207.

[3] R. O. Faulkner, "Egypt: From the Inception of the Nineteenth Dynasty to the Death of Ramses III," *CAH*[3] II/2 Cambridge 1975) 234.

[4] The occurrence of the name Israel here alongside the common terms Hatti, Canaan, and Kharu may indicate that it is much older than the reign of Merneptah.

[5] See Faulkner, "Egypt," 234. S. Yeivin, among others, has suggested that this campaign took place in Merneptah's third year, which would explain the brief description here, which seems to highlight only a few points; see Yeivin, *The Israelite Conquest of Canaan* (İstanbul Nederlands Historisch-Archaeologisch Instituut in het Nabije Oosten 27; Leiden, 1971) 30. See also the discussion of H. Engel, "Die Siegesstele des Merneptah," *Biblica* 60 (1979) 373–99. For a different approach establishing the genuineness of Merneptah's Syro-Palestinian campaign, see Frank Yurco, "Merneptah's Palestinian Campaign," *The Society for the Study of Egyptian Antiquities Journal* 8 (1982) 70. Here we could also note that W. G. Dever and D. P. Cole have associated the destruction (by fire) of stratum XV at Gezer with Merneptah's campaign. The pottery of the following stratum XIV is Canaanite and thus it may have been built by Gezerites who returned to the site; later the Philistines took over the place (W. G. Dever et al., *Gezer II: Report of the 1967–70 Seasons in Field I and II* [Jerusalem, 1974] 50).

[6] While Egyptian campaigns seldom went up into the hill country in the centuries before Merneptah, it is possible that his campaign needed to subdue the growing population of the hills. On the other hand, he may have encountered "Israel" in the lowland areas as allies of the Canaanites,

As I have already pointed out elsewhere,[7] the coda section has the following ring structure:

The princes are prostrate and say "Peace"	A
Not one raises his head among the Nine Bows.	
Desolation is for Tehenu; Hatti is pacified;	B
Plundered is Canaan with every evil	C
Carried off is Ashkelon,	D
Siezed upon is Gezer,	D_1
Yeno^{c}am is made as that which does not exist	D_2
Israel is laid waste, his seed is not;	C_1
Kharu has become a widow because of Egypt.[8]	B_1
All lands together are pacified;	A_1
Everyone who was restless has been bound	
by the King of Upper and Lower Egypt:	
Ba-en-Re Meri-Amon; the Son of Re:	
Mer-ne-Ptah Hotep-hir-Maat, given life	
like Re every day.[9]	

We should note that the formal structure pairs Hatti with Kharu, Canaan with Israel, and groups Gezer, Ashkelon, and Yeno^{c}am together. Each of these groupings in turn defines a more precise geographical territory: Hatti and Kharu stand for the whole area of Syria-Palestine; Canaan and Israel represent the smaller unit Palestine; and finally, within this area, we find the three specific city-states. I favor viewing the component elements in each group as complementary subdivisions rather than as rough synonyms,[10] so that Canaan and Israel would be subdivisions of the greater

---

banding together to fight a common enemy. Cf. also H. Y. Priebutsch, "Jerusalem und die Brunnenstrasse Merneptahs," *ZDPV* 91 (1975) 18ff.

[7] G. W. Ahlström and D. Edelman, "Merneptah's Israel," *JNES* 44 (1985) 59–61.

[8] The preposition *n* (which usually is dative) should be translated here as 'because of' (E. F. Wente, oral communication).

[9] For the full text, see J. A. Wilson, *ANET*, 376–78; G. Fecht, "Die Israelstele, Gestalt und Aussage," in *Fontes atque Pontes: Eine Festgabe für Hellmut Brunner* (Ägypten und Altes Testament 5; ed. M. Görg; Wiesbaden, 1983) 106–38, and (in the same volume), E. Hornung, "Die Israelstele des Merneptah," 224–33.

[10] Ahlström and Edelman, "Merneptah's Israel," 59–61.

area Palestine. Remembering that in its extended meaning Canaan referred to the cultural and urban areas of the country,[11] the name Israel logically refers to the remaining sparsely populated hill country area where few cities were located (fig. 1).

In this case, it would be natural to see the peoples living in the hills as being known as Israelites far back in time,[12] and thus, Israel could originally have been the name of a territory, i.e., the hill country. The use of the determinative for people with the name rather than the one for a foreign land does not necessarily contradict this proposal. Biblical scholars have generally blown the determinative issue out of proportion. Egyptologists attach little significance to the choice of determinative here, recognizing that determinatives were generally used rather loosely by scribes, especially when a people was called by the name of the territory they inhabited. If Israel was a territorial name, it cannot be argued that a pre-existing group called Israel moved into the hill country region, because outside of the territory of Israel, there were no Israelites. Therefore, the theory that the name Israel stood for a new tribal society created in the hills,[13] cannot be accepted.

The possible origin of Israel as a territorial name would explain why in the Amarna texts, Labayu's kingdom, which was based at Shechem but which appears to have controlled only a portion of the central hill country, was never called Israel. Since it did not include the whole hill country area, it would not have been referred to by the territorial name Israel. It was with the emergence of Saul's kingdom that the name Israel first came to signify a political entity.

The use of the name Israel on the Merneptah stele, therefore, cannot be cited as proof that the biblical Israel left Egypt and settled in Canaan. This idea is part of a theological reconstruction from a time much later than the Merneptah

[11] Num 13:29; Josh 5:1; Isa 23:11, for instance. For a general history of the term, see de Vaux, *The Early History of Israel*, 125ff.

[12] This would nullify Helck's guess that Israel refers here to a great nomadic people which had invaded Palestine (*Die Beziehungen*, 224).

[13] N. P. Lemche, "'Hebrew' as a National Name for Israel," 7.

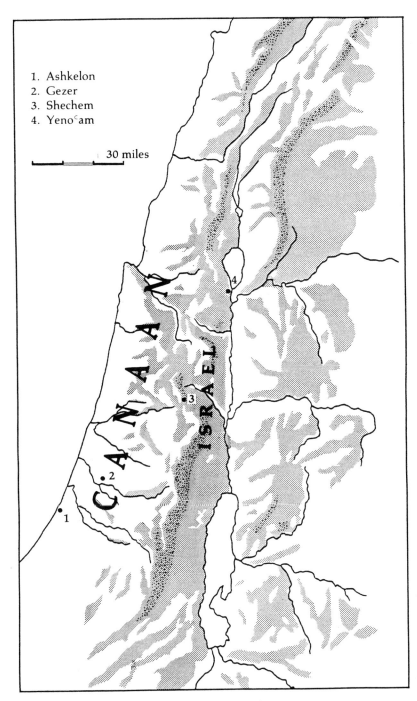

1. Ashkelon
2. Gezer
3. Shechem
4. Yeno‘am

30 miles

Fig. 1 Palestine according to Merneptah's stela.

inscription. In fact, the biblical writers did not seem to know anything about an Israelite defeat by the Egyptians before the Solomonic period. The Merneptah stele cannot be used, therefore, as Y. Aharoni maintains,[14] to fix the date of the Israelite conquest.

In light of my proposal that the name Israel was used for most of the hill country, what did the term Judah originally stand for? There is no consensus on this point. J. Hempel thought it might be a short form of yěhûd-ʾēl ("gepreisen sei El"),[15] while H. S. Nyberg considered it to be a deity name, which was then extended to a territory[16] as was somewhat common in the Semitic world (cf. the names Ashur and Edom, and possibly even Yahweh).[17] A. Alt suggested that Judah was originally a place name.[18] Although this is possible, it is more probable, as R. de Vaux has proposed, that it was a territorial or regional name which gave its name to the people who lived there[19] and thus also, to the later "tribe" of Judah. Therefore, the phrase har yěhûdāh "the mountain region of Judah," in Josh 20:7, could be an old common term for the southern hills.[20]

It seems probable that the name Judah, like that of Israel, originally referred to a territory. However, the two names were probably not parallel. Israel probably designated the

[14] Aharoni, The Land of the Bible, 184.

[15] "Juda," Biblisch-Historisches Handwörterbuch II (ed. L. Rost and B. Reicke; Göttingen, 1964) 898.

[16] H. S. Nyberg, Studien zum Hoseabuche (UUÅ 1935:6), p. 77.

[17] The Shosu territory yahwaʾ may be named after Yahweh; cf. de Vaux, The Early History of Israel, 334.

[18] A. Alt, "Der Gott der Väter," KS I (Munich, 1953) 5, n. 1. He is followed by M. Noth, Die Welt des Alten Testaments (Berlin, 1953) 50f.; de Vaux, The Early History of Israel, 547. E. Lipiński ("L'étymologie de 'Juda'," VT 23 [1973] 380f.) derives yěhûd from the root whd (Arabic wahda, 'gorge, ravine'). The failure of this root to appear in biblical Hebrew does not mean that it did not exist in Hebrew-Canaanite. This theory would support Judah's territorial nature.

[19] de Vaux, The Early History of Israel, 547. Cf. S. Mowinckel, Tetrateuch-Pentateuch-Hexateuch (BZAW 90; Berlin, 1964) 66.

[20] M. Noth compares this with the phrase har ʾeprayîm, 'the mountain region of Ephraim,' and considers both to be names of lands rather than tribes (Das Buch Josua [HAT 7; Tübingen, 1953] 126).

whole hill country. Judah, on the other hand, is always limited in scope to the hill country region south of Bethlehem and extends down to the Negev. Therefore, it appears to be a subdivisional unit within Israel whose northern counterpart is Ephraim. With this in mind, David probably did not invent the name Judah for his newly created kingdom. Rather, he converted the old geographical term for the territory of his new kingdom into a political name.

5

The Role of the Sea:
Mythological Historiography

One result of the Egyptian campaigns in Syria-Palestine was the transportation of Semitic captives to Egypt for use as slaves.[1] In texts from the 19th and 20th dynasties, for instance, Semitic slaves are mentioned as workers who were used to build cities and monumental edifices. This fact has often been used to confirm the statement in Exod 1:1ff. that the Hebrews were slaves in Egypt and were used for forced labor to build the cities of Pithom and Raamses. The Egyptian texts, however, do not prove anything specific about the Israelites;[2] they only show that the biblical writer knew a tradition about the use of Semites in forced labor in Egypt. Such knowledge must have been well known in Palestine for generations. Nevertheless, it is possible that the memory of a sojourn in Egypt was kept alive in the central Israelite hill country by Semites who had succeeded in escaping there

---

[1] See, for instance, the inscription of Amenhotep II's campaign, Helck, *Die Beziehungen*, 344; J. A. Wilson, *ANET*, 246f.

[2] J. Bright states categorically that even if "there is no direct witness in Egyptian records to Israel's presence in Egypt, the Biblical tradition a priori demands belief" (*A History of Israel*, 121). No historian could accept such a statement. For the location of the Egyptian cities Avaris and Piramesse (which is not Tanis) in the eastern Delta at Tell el-Dabᶜa and Qantir, see M. Bietak, "Avaris and Piramesse: Archaeological Explorations in the Eastern Nile Delta," *Proceedings of the British Academy* 65 (London, 1979) 271ff., 278ff.

from Egypt. Later during the exile in Babylonia and the problems of the return to Palestine, a biblical historiographer was able to use the bondage in Egypt as the starting point in his reconstruction of the history of Yahweh's people by transforming it into a pan-Israelite experience.

Given the fact that Asiatic peoples were in Egypt as intruders or as prisoners of war and slaves, we cannot ignore the possible inclusion of the expulsion of the Hyksos (16th century B.C.) in the source material which was available for literary activities. One may assume that the Hyksos experience was retold in different ways and in different circles through time. This is not to say that the Hyksos expulsion should be identified with the story about the Israelites leaving Egypt. However, the Hyksos event could have been part of the folklore or common tradition which the biblical narrator used for background and flavor. He did not make his story an expulsion from Egypt but an escape, and it was not a ruling class which had to leave, but a bunch of slaves who ran away.[3] We should note in the Exodus story that not only Hebrews, but also other peoples with them, left Egypt (Exod 12:38), which suggests a common knowledge about the presence of several Asiatic groups in Egypt and their exit or escape from there. Thus, we conclude that many exoduses from Egypt occurred in the course of history.

Since the biblical text is concerned primarily with divine actions, which are not verifiable, it is impossible to use the exodus story as a source to reconstruct the history of the Late Bronze and Early Iron I periods. The text is concerned with mythology rather than with a detailed reporting of historical facts. As soon as someone "relates" a god's actions or words, mythology has been written. On the other hand, the exodus account is an interesting literary source for the history of ideas. The exodus and the consequent wanderings in the wilderness are part of a historiographic chain of

---

[3] For the material culture of the Canaanite-Asiatic community in the Eastern Delta during the MB II period, see Bietak, "Avaris and Piramesse," 272ff., and J. S. Holladay, *Cities of the Delta III: Tell el-Maskhuṭa* (American Research Center in Egypt, Reports Vol. 6; Malibu, CA, 1982) 44–47.

happenings and traditions whose purpose is to link Israel's history with prehistoric time as far back as the dawn of time and the creation of the cosmos, as it was understood.[4] Such historiography frequently uses mythological terms and motifs because the history being described is governed by divine actions. A good illustration of this is the motif of *yam*, 'the Sea,' i.e., the mythological adversary, or of *mayim rabbîm*, 'the many waters,' a variant form. This motif occurs in several psalms,[5] in the Exodus narratives, in the story of the crossing of the river Jordan, and in the story of Sisera's battle against the Canaanites.

The Exodus story relates Yahweh's divine actions: how he let his people leave Egypt, the land of bondage, and then how he saved them from the pursuing Egyptians through the wonder of the Sea, *yam sûp*.[6] The text focuses on the

---

[4] This idea is known elsewhere in the ancient Near East. For example, Egyptian "history" begins with *tatenen*, the primeval hill, rising out of the water, followed by a quick shift of interest to Egypt, its gods and peoples. In this religious thought pattern, however, Egypt is identified with the cosmos. For *tatenen*, see, among others, A. Erman, *Die Religion der Ägypter* (Berlin and Leipzig, 1934) 25, 89; J. Černy, *Ancient Egyptian Religion* (London, 1952) 44; S. Morenz, *Ägyptische Religion* (Die Religionen der Menschheit 8; Stuttgart, 1960) 45; and E. Hornung, *Der Eine und die Vielen* (Darmstadt, 1971) 71.

[5] H. G. May, "Some Cosmic Connotations of *Mayim Rabbîm*, Many Waters," *JBL* 74 (1955) 9–21; cf. G. W. Ahlström, *Psalm 89* (Lund, 1959) 67ff.; O. Kaiser, *Die mythische Bedeutung des Meeres in Ägypten, Ugarit und Israel* (BZAW 78; Berlin, 1959) 141ff. For Ugaritic parallels, see also A. S. Kapelrud, *Baal in the Ras Shamra Texts* (Copenhagen, 1952) 98–112; and M. K. Wakeman, *God's Battle with the Monster* (Leiden, 1973) 92–102.

[6] S. Norin maintains that the Elephantine finds, though fragmentary, indicate that the Passover became linked to the escape from Egypt (the Exodus) and that the exact date of the festival was fixed at a late point in the religion of Israel. He also maintains that "allem Anschein nach haben sich also in Elephantine die alten kultischen Überlieferungen erhalten, die zwischen *paesäḥ* und *mǎṣṣôt* ein unterschied machten, die beiden Feste nicht exakt datieren und sie nicht mit dem Auszug verbanden" (*Er Spaltete das Meer* [ConB OT Ser. 9; Lund, 1977] 188f.). He concludes that none of the psalms he has dealt with (18, 29, 33, 66, 74, 77, 78, 80, 81, 89, 105, 106, 111, 114, 118, 124, 135) show that the Exodus tradition was used in the Jerusalem cultus at the time of the division of Solomon's kingdom (pp. 195f.). A discussion of all of these psalms is not necessary here; only

divine deed expressed through the *yam sûp* incident and the splitting of the sea, rather than on historical reality. Since the story is not to be understood as a historical event in the modern sense of the term, it is doubtful that an exodus event is being related. Just as Genesis 1 explains how the cosmos came into being through the will of the god, so the story of the exodus tells how the people of Yahweh (i.e., the people Israel—this is the religious use of the name) came into existence. Exodus 1–15 can be called a "creation story" of the people of Yahweh and should not be used as a modern historiographical textbook. The historical details are deliberately out of focus; they are irrelevant. For the biblical narrator, as for other Near Eastern writers, the gods steered the course of events, so that his creation account needed only the sheen of history. Ancient Near Eastern historiography was expressed in mythological categories because the gods were the lords of history.[7]

Psalms 78 and 89 will be considered. Psalm 78 is a poem with a historic retrospect and, as such, cannot be early. It uses, for instance, the verb *bq*ᶜ, 'to split' (v 13) to describe Yahweh's dealings with the waters, as does Neh 9:11, for the same event. This could indicate that the idea of the splitting of the sea is late, and probably post-exilic. In Psalm 89, the *yam* motif is oriented more cosmologically than towards a depiction of the Exodus event. This is to be expected since the hymn describes the god's cosmological and world-wide rule. It nevertheless is understandable that the motifs of *yam* and Rahab in Ps 89:9[10]f. have been understood by some to be references to the Exodus event because they also appear in the Exodus story. See also C. Petersen, *Mythos im Alten Testament: Bestimmung des Mythosbegriffs und Untersuchung der mythischen Element in den Psalmen* (BZAW 157; Berlin and New York, 1982) 142f., 166–76.

[7] Cf. for instance, B. Albrektson, *History and the Gods* (ConB OT Ser. 1; Lund, 1967). It should be emphasized that religions often depict events as being rooted in the divine will. We should also note the role of the Egyptian priesthood in historiography and "Wissenschaft." See, for example, S. Sauneron, *Les prêtres de l'ancienne Egypte* (Paris, 1957) 111–27 (Engl. tr. A. Morrisset, *The Priest of Ancient Egypt* [London, 1960] 113ff.). Possibly the historiography of Israel and Judah also began with priestly writings about the mythical acts of the divine world. For the role of mythology in poetry, cf. J. Fränkel, who says that the poet creates "kosmisch-religiöse Mythen, in denen das religiöse Fühlen des Volkes symbolisiert wird. Denn die

The passing through of the *yam sûp* (the so-called "Red Sea event") represents a special literary use of a mythological idea to describe the ideological birth of the people Israel. The translations "Red Sea" or "Sea of Reeds" are misunderstandings of the phrase which are rooted in an attempt to historicize the story. The Hebrew word *sûp* means "end," so that the *yam sûp* would be best translated "Sea of Destruction," with *sûp* expressing the mythological function of the waters.[8] In Hebrew mythology, the mythical waters of chaos often appear as Yahweh's enemy. After conquering them, Yahweh places his throne on the waters and rules over them (cf. Ps 89:9[10]).[9] In the Exodus narrative the *yam* was subdued by Yahweh's command and was split so that the people could pass through and be saved from disaster. When the Egyptian army tried to do the same, the waters were allowed to return to their old function and drowned the enemy.[10] Thanks to the will of the god, the enemy went to the realm of destruction and death. Because of the mythological nature of the *yam sûp*, it is impossible to locate it geographically just as it is impossible to locate the mountains which were melted when Yahweh walked on them (Judg 5:5).[11]

The psalm in Exod 15:1–18 emphasizes the mythological character of the exodus event. It glorifies Yahweh's actions

---

Religion hat keine andere Sprache als den Mythus" (*Dichtung und Wissenschaft* [Heidelberg, 1954] 28). A poet perhaps often used old myths which were priestly expressions of the nation's religion.

[8] Cf. my "Another Moses Tradition," 65ff.; and B. F. Batto, "The Reed Sea: Requiescat in Pace," *JBL* 102 (1983) 27ff.; de Vaux, *The Early History of Israel*, 377.

[9] For these concepts, see my *Psalm 89*, 69ff.

[10] Cf. J. Pedersen, *Israel* III–IV (London, 1949) 728ff.; O. Eissfeldt, "Gott und das Meer in der Bibel," in *Studia Orientalia Ioanni Pedersen* (Copenhagen, 1953) 78f.; I. Engnell, *A Rigid Scrutiny* (ed. J. T. Willis; Nashville, 1969) 197f. The process of the historicization of the myth had already begun in the time of the biblical writers, since Ezion-Geber is said to be "near Elath on the shore of *yam sûp* in the land of Edom" in 1 Kgs 9:26.

[11] J. Pedersen, *Israel* III–IV, 728ff.

for his people. It is impossible to use the poem as a source for historiography in the modern sense of the term and it is difficult to draw any conclusions about its date. Nonetheless, according to F. M. Cross[12] and D. N. Freedman who follows him, this is allegedly one of the oldest, if not the oldest, texts of the Hebrew Bible. Freedman goes so far as to date it to "the last quarter of the 13th century, while a preferable date would be around 1200, or very early in the twelfth century."[13] Freedman's date assigns the poem to a time from which no Hebrew script is known. For Cross, the text is a "primary source for the central event in Israel's history, the Exodus-Conquest,"[14]—an event which, as discussed above, probably did not occur as related in the texts.

The content of the poem can be late just as well as early. The description of Yahweh's throne and temple suggests a post-Solomonic date. Freedman is forced to conclude that these refer to the heavenly temple rather than a man-made one in order to be consistent with his early date. But in order for a poet to describe a heavenly temple he must first have been familiar with the earthly phenomenon since, psychologically speaking, heavenly objects are projections of earthly, human experiences. No *Israelite* national temple existed as the center for Yahweh's official cult before the temple of Solomon was built (excluding from consideration the house/temple of Yahweh in Jerusalem mentioned in 2 Sam 12:20 and the *bāmāh*, 'sanctuary,' at Gibeon). Freedman has not understood the ideological reality of a temple. It represents heaven on earth and the god's heavenly and earthly domain, which are one in his temple.[15] As

[12] F. M. Cross, *Canaanite Myth and Hebrew Epic* (Cambridge, MA, 1973) 123ff.

[13] D. N. Freedman, "Early Israelite History in the Light of Early Israelite Poetry," in *Unity and Diversity: Essays in History, Literature, and Religion of the Ancient Near East* (ed. H. Goedicke and J. J. M. Roberts; Baltimore, 1975) 5ff., 10.

[14] Cross, *Canaanite Myth*, 123. If one takes the Exodus event as the primary focus of Judahite religion, one could agree.

[15] For temple ideology in the Near East, see G. W. Ahlström, "Heaven on Earth at Hazor and Arad," in *Religious Syncretism in Antiquity* (ed. B. A. Pearson; Missoula, MT, 1975) 67–83.

A. Erman has pointed out, the temple is the "heilige Stätte der Urzeit."[16] It is because of this that the descriptions of its god(s) and his/their divine actions are timeless, original, new, and yet at the same time primeval, "uralt."

We should note that the content of the song in Exodus 15 does not agree with the events as related in the prose version of the crossing of the sea. Cross also has noticed this, and states that there is no mention of the "splitting of the sea or of the east wind blowing the waters back so the Israelites can cross," or of the waters returning and causing the Egyptians to drown. Instead, there is "a storm-tossed sea that is directed against the Egyptians."[17] Here the mythological waters (Exod 15:8) have been used to give added weight to the divine wonder. Consequently, we may have to posit the existence of different traditions concerning the "sea wonder." The splitting of the sea could be later than the Exodus 15 song, or it could belong to another tradition.

A relatively late date for Exodus 15 is probable in light of a number of details and considerations. It is noteworthy that the use of the expression *yam sûp* for the sea of the exodus is elsewhere characteristic of deuteronomistic and post-deuteronomistic texts.[18] Other texts use simply *yam*, and it is probable that *sûp* is an Aramean word "introduced into Hebrew at a late date."[19] Exod 15:17f. also expresses an idea found in later biblical tradition: the place Yahweh has chosen, the mountain of his inheritance, which is the temple

---

[16] A. Erman, *Die Religion der Ägypter* (Berlin and Leipzig, 1934) 89.

[17] Cross, *Canaanite Myth*, 131. Exodus 15 may be seen as a version of the old Canaanite myth about the battle between the storm and the sea. See E. L. Greenstein, "The Snaring of the Sea in the Baal Epic," *Maarav* 3 (1982) 195ff.

[18] See Norin, *Er Spaltete das Meer*, 33, 94. He argues that the exodus from Egypt is not associated with either the *pesaḥ* or *maṣṣôt* festival in the P and J material. It is the deuteronomistic tradition which links these festivals with the exit from Egypt and fixes the celebration's date to the month of Abib (pp. 182ff., 198, 206). Cf. J. Van Seters who states that J has no passover story ("The Place of the Yahwist in the History of Passover and Massot," *ZAW* 95 [1983] 167–82).

[19] de Vaux, *The Early History*, 377.

mount of Jerusalem in biblical tradition.[20] Verse 13 seems to be a further allusion to the temple, with its reference to Yahweh's leading of the people "to your holy dwelling" (ʾel nĕwēh qodšekā. Hebrew nwh, which normally refers to pasture land and sometimes also to steppe land, is used in certain contexts as a term for a dwelling place. In Prov 3:33, 21:20 and Job 5:3, for instance, it signifies 'house.' In light of the characterization of Yahweh as the shepherd of his people, nwh has been used to designate Yahweh's dwelling place, Jerusalem (2 Sam 15:25; Jer 25:30; 31:23).[21] Putting the expression nĕwēh qodšekā (v 13) alongside the phrase mākôn lĕšibtĕkā, "the (cult) place where you (i.e., you throne) sit" (v 17), it becomes clear that the song is referring to an earthly temple, most probably Jerusalem (cf. 1 Kgs 8:13).

Two final points can be mentioned which tend to suggest a date of composition later than 1200 B.C. Verse 14 refers to the "pangs" which had "taken hold of the inhabitants of Philistia." This inclusion of the Philistines must date from a point in time in which they had had sufficient time to build up and consolidate their position in southern Palestine so as to become a threat to the rest of the peoples of Palestine.[22] 1200 B.C. is too early for this. In addition, it is to be observed

[20] S. Mowinckel, "Psalm Criticism Between 1900 and 1935 (Ugarit and Psalm Exegesis)," VT 5 (1955) 13–33. Cross has tried to use Ugaritic texts to explain the phrase "mount of possession," (or "inheritance") concluding that it refers to the whole hill country, the territory of the god, and that the poem therefore is older than the Jerusalem period (Canaanite Myth, 125). This could actually be an argument for the text's late date. N. C. Habel thinks that "Canaan is his throne," while seeing at the same time that the idea of the mount of inheritance is "connected with the rule of Yahweh from his central sanctuary" (Yahweh versus Baal: A Conflict of Religious Cultures [New York, 1964] 62). From the Ugaritic parallels M. Metzger draws the conclusion that the temple in Exodus 15 refers to the god mountain at Jerusalem ("Himmlischer und iridische Wohnstadt Jahwes," UF 2 [1970] 147, n. 27).

[21] Cf. J. Obermann, "An Antiphonal Psalm from Ras Shamra," JBL 55 (1936) 38, n. 36; I. Engnell, "Planted by the Streams of Water," Studia Orientalia Ioanni Pedersen (Copenhagen, 1953) 95. For the Akkadian cognate signifying the place where cattle and sheep can find pasture, see, among others, D. O. Edzard, "Altbabylonisch nawûm," ZA 53 (1959) 168f.

[22] The religious focus of the text seems to have escaped Freedman, cf. n. 13. His interpretation, like others, seems to be due to an unquestioning

that Exodus 15 is composed in the style of a royal psalm.[23] It ends with the typical phrase *yhwh mlk l⁽lm w⁽d*, "Yahweh reigns forever and ever," and is written in the typical Near Eastern royal style which uses the first person singular pronoun, the "royal I," to celebrate the victories in hymnic form.[24] The Song of the Sea cannot be much older than the literary composition detailing the Exodus and Wilderness Wandering which it glorifies.[25] In this glorification the poet has used the very ancient Semitic motif of the dangerous sea.

The water motif found in the Exodus event is used in the same way in Joshua 3, in the story of the people's crossing the Jordan. Yahweh stopped the water so that it stood up as a wall, making it possible for the people to walk on "dry" land over to Cisjordan. It did not matter to the author of this narrative that the Jordan was and continues to be a shallow river with several accessible fords. His primary goal was to characterize the entry to the promised land as a supernatural event directed by his god.[26]

---

acceptance of the story of the biblical Exodus as historical fact. Cross thinks that the Philistines could have been part of the Sea Peoples' attack on Egypt under Ramses II and Merneptah (*Canaanite Myth*, 124ff.). As far as is known, the Philistines participated in an assault on Egypt for the first time in the reign of Ramses III (1182–1151). Ramses II would have reigned from 1279 to 1212 and his son Merneptah from 1212–1202, according to the chronology developed by E. F. Wente and C. van Siclen ("A Chronology of the New Kingdom," *Studies in Honor of George R. Hughes* [SAOC 39; Chicago, 1976] 217–61).

23 Cf. K. Rendtorff, "Sejrshymnen i Exodus 15 og dens forhold til tronbestigelsessalmerne," *DTT* 22 (1959) 65ff., 156ff.

24 Cf. S. Mowinckel, *The Psalms in Israel's Worship* (2 vols., trans. D. R. Ap-Thomas; New York and Nashville, 1962) 71ff. It is impossible to say whether the writer has used an old psalm or composed a new one in the style of a royal psalm. G. Beer and K. Galling think that Exodus 15 could have been composed as a "Passahkantate" for Josiah's new Passover festival in 621 B.C., 2 Kgs 23:21ff. (*Exodus* [HAT; Tübingen, 1939] 84).

25 G. W. Coats, for instance, maintains that the *yam sûp* motif "rarely appears in pre-Exilic texts" ("The Traditio-Historical Character of the Reed Sea Motif," *VT* 17 [1967] 262).

26 F. M. Cross has connected Exodus 15 with a cult ceremony at Gilgal after the conquest ("The Song of the Sea and Canaanite Myth," *JTC* 5 [1968] 1–25). The mythic character of this story, coupled with the

In the Song of Deborah in Judges 5 we again find waters drowning Israel's enemies. Here it is reported that the heavenly host (i.e., deities) were fighting and that the Kishon River flooded, drowning the entire enemy army except Sisera, who was running away! But how could he run away on water? Again, mythology has been used to describe an event which the writer wanted to anchor in the will of Yahweh. This is part of the poetic imagery. As is common when mythological motifs are employed, history almost disappears from this poem. One piece of information which may record historical fact is the report that only the peoples of Naphtali and Zebulon risked their lives in the battle (v 18). This is supported by the prose version in Judges 4 which only mentions these two tribes, suggesting that the conflict only involved peoples of the north. Long after the battle, a poet wrote about the events of the days of Deborah and Jael and composed his "song" from a pan-Israelite viewpoint.[27] We should note further that Judg 4:16 states that Barak pursued the chariots and the army of the Canaanites and that they "all fell by the sword, not one man was left." According to this text, there was no flooding. The claim that no enemy survived the battle is a common Near Eastern practice of exaggerating military victories. The primary intent of the prose account and the poetic account seems to be to show that the victory was guided by the will of Yahweh.

In the texts examined, the mythological water/sea motif has been used to express the interventionary power of the divine will. The motif has been made part of a literary construction in order to lay claim to the country in a time

---

fictional nature of the conquest, makes this suggestion improbable. R. Hulst sees Joshua 3 as a "Sondertradition" which was brought into connection with the stories about the conquest ("Der Jordan in den alttestamentlichen Überlieferungen," Oudtestamentische Studiën 14 [Leiden, 1965] 168–84).

[27] For the date of Judges 5, cf. G. W. Ahlström, "Judges 5:20f. and History," JNES 36 (1977) 287ff. We should note that neither Barak nor Deborah are said to have saved Israel, which may explain why they are not mentioned in 1 Sam 12:8ff.

when the right to the land was disputed. In this fictional historiography[28] the twelve tribes miraculously escaped from Egypt, the land of bondage, and after forty years of "Wanderings in the Wilderness" (a period of purification and stabilization of the society), they crossed the Jordan, a shallow river, and then conquered Canaan. This sequence is definitely not one of empirical history.

[28] For the role of myth in Hebrew historiography, see G. Widengren, "Myth and History in Israelite-Jewish Thought," in *Culture in History: Essays in Honor of Paul Radin* (ed. S. Diamond; New York, 1960) 467–95.

6

The Peoples of the Territory Israel

We have seen that the demographic picture of ancient Palestine changed somewhat in the wake of the upheavals in the eastern Mediterranean in the 13th and 12th centuries B.C. The central hills saw an increase in population, with many new villages built on unoccupied sites. As has been pointed out, the archaeological remains show that the material culture of these new settlements is mainly Canaanite, and it is therefore unwise to advocate that a new ethnic group with a different culture and lifestyle invaded the hills. Nor is there any indication to date of a concerted military conquest of the area. The available evidence tends to suggest that most of the settlers arrived from the cultural and urban centers of Canaan, i.e., from the territories of the city-states in the west and north. In addition, it is likely that groups originating in the east and south also penetrated the hills. There are reminiscences of this in the Old Testament. The Ammonites, for instance, are said to have expanded into the Jericho area (Judg 3:13f.), and the Amalekites appear to have settled in the hills of Ephraim (Judg 12:15). Presumably, the Ammonite expansion and pressure in the periods of Jephthah and Saul was preceded by an attempt by some Ammonite groups to get a foothold in Cisjordan.

Among other incoming groups were the Midianites, who seem to have settled south and west of Lake Tiberias (Judg 4:17ff.; 5:6, 24ff.; Josh 19:33). Gideon's war against the Midianites is reported to have taken place in the territory of

Issachar, which was a non-Israelite area at that time.[1] The Midianite penetration into Cisjordanian territories can be seen not only as an example of peoples seeking new "pastures," but also as one of conflicts of interests leading to wars between the different communities.[2]

Several Edomite clans were among groups which moved into the hills from the south. The Calebites, the Kenites, the Jerahmeelites, and the Kenizzites[3] can be named (cf. Num 13:6; 32:12; Josh 24:6ff.; Judg 1:12ff.; 1 Sam 27:10; 30:29).[4] In light of the claim of biblical tradition that Yahweh came from Seir, Paran, and Teman, all names of districts in Edom,[5] it is appropriate to ask whether one of these groups arrived with a god called Yahweh. As already mentioned, the phrase "Yahweh of Teman and his Asherah" from Kuntillet ʿAjrud (ca. 800 B.C.) confirms an Edomite provenience for Yahweh and, in addition, indicates his possession of a consort.[6]

---

[1] Issachar is not mentioned in the list of the peoples who fought with Gideon. See Elizabeth J. Payne, "The Midianite Arc in Joshua and Judges," in *Midian, Moab, and Edom: The History and Archaeology of Late Bronze and Iron Age Jordan and North-West Arabia* (JSOT Suppl. Ser. 24; ed. F. J. A. Sawyer and D. J. A. Clines; Sheffield, 1983) 166f. E. A. Knauf concludes that the Midianites were "a sedentary and agricultural society, employing terrace farming and other irrigation techniques" in the wadis of North Arabia. The breakdown of the Late Bronze culture led to the invasion of some raiding parties into Palestine ("Midianites and Ishmaelites," in *Midian, Moab, and Edom*, 151).

[2] Gideon is said in Judges 8 to have pushed the Midianites out of the country into Ammonite territory in Transjordan. Cf. H. M. Orlinsky, "The Tribal System of Israel and Related Groups in the Period of the Judges," *Oriens Antiquus* 1 (1962) 18f.

[3] In Num 32:12, Caleb is made a descendant of the Kenizzites. In Gen 36:11, 15, Kenaz is the son of Esau, i.e., Edom.

[4] The genealogical list in 1 Chr 2:50−55 relates the Kenites to the Calebites and Rechabites.

[5] Paran is usually identified with the territory south of the eastern Negev in the Sinai, and Teman is probably the most eastern part of Edom. Seir is usually a parallel name used for Edom, east of the Arabah, cf. Gen 14:6.

[6] Cf. below, pp. 92f.; and my *An Archaeological Picture of Iron Age Religions in Ancient Palestine* (Studia Orientalia 55/3; Helsinki, 1984) 18−21.

In the theophanic hymn of Judges 5, Yahweh is said to "come forth from Seir" and to "march forth from the fields of Edom" (v 4), while in Deut 33:2 he is described as shining forth from Sinai and showing himself in his splendor from the mountainous region of Paran (cf. Hab 3:3). The theophanic description begins with a statement of the deity's original home, so far as is known. Wherever he is worshiped, he is still the god who shines forth from Seir, Paran, Teman. Therefore, his holy mountain Sinai must have been located somewhere in that area.

As a territorial god, the land over which he ruled could have been known also by his own name following the common Semitic practice (cf. Ashur, Edom, Ashtartu, and Anath).[7] With this in mind, we should examine the often-quoted phrases which occur in Egyptian lists of the New Kingdom period, *š3sw yhw*ʾ and *š3sw s*ʾ*rr*, i.e., the territories *yhw*ʾ and *s*ʾ*rr*. According to Helck, the verb *š3š* means 'to wander around'; thus, the term *š3św* (Shasu) would refer to bedouins.[8]

Egyptian *s*ʾ*rr* has usually been identified with Hebrew *śē*ᶜ*ir* and has been understood as a reference to Seir-Edom. This, however, is doubtful. M. Astour has pointed out that the Egyptian spelling *s*ʾ*rr* does not correspond to Hebrew *s*ᶜ*r*.[9] He also has shown that Shasu people were found in Lebanon, Syria, and northern Palestine, all areas where the Egyptians campaigned. The list in Ramses II's temple at

---

[7] Consult, for instance, J. Lewy, "Les textes paléo-assyriens et l'Ancien Testament," *Revue de l'histoire des religions* 110 (1934) 43–49; M. Astour, "Yahweh in Egyptian Topographical Lists," *Festschrift Elmar Edel 12. Märtz 1979* (Ägypten und Altes Testament 1; ed. M. Görg and E. Pusch; Bamberg, 1979) 30, n. 71; cf. also E. Täubler, *Biblische Studien: Die Epoche der Richter* (ed. H.-J. Zobel; Tübingen, 1958) 116.

[8] Helck, *Die Beziehungen*, 274. See R. Giveon, *Les bédouins Shosu des documents égyptiens* (Leiden, 1971); J. Leclant, *Les fouilles de Soleb (Nubie soudanaise): Quelques remarques sur les écussons des peuples envoûtés de la salle hypostyle du secteur IV* (Nachrichten der Akad. der Wissenschaften, Phil.-hist. Klasse; Göttingen, 1965) 214ff. Cf. de Vaux, *The Early History of Israel*, 334; Herrmann, *A History of Israel*, 76f. For the characteristics of the Shasu people in the pictographic art, see Giveon, *Les bédouins*, 241–58.

[9] Astour, "Yahweh in Egyptian Topographical Lists," 17–33.

ᶜAmārah in Sudan names the Beqaᶜ, Orontes, and Eleu-
therus valleys in Lebanon and Syria as Shasu territories. It is
in this context that *šꜣsw yhwꜣ* is mentioned, which must
mean that it also belongs to the Beqaᶜ-Orontes districts.[10]
The Shasu peoples have been catalogued in the Egyptian
topographical lists by the places where they camped. From
this we can conclude that the name *yhwꜣ* is used as a
toponym in these texts. We cannot conclude that it also
referred to a deity, even though "in the ancient Near East
many anthroponyms could serve as toponyms,"[11] and the
same could be the case with deity names, as mentioned
above.

From all this it should be clear that the above-mentioned
Egyptian references to the Shasu *yhwꜣ* cannot be used to
support the biblical tradition of Yahweh's coming from
Edom, which is attested in such different texts as Judges,
Habakkuk, and Deuteronomy. To these can be added the
tradition that Jacob (i.e., Israel) is Edom's younger twin (cf.
Gen 25:21–30); thus, a southeastern provenience seems to
be undeniable. For the origin of Yahweh himself, we still
cannot get behind the Hebrew textual material. Everything
else becomes speculation, even though it is probable that
Edom originally was settled from the north.

Among the peoples of Canaan, the Danites are of con-
siderable interest. According to the Bible, they lived in the
area between Aijalon, Ir-Shemesh, and Joppa, which was
close to the Philistines. According to Josh 19:43, the two
Philistine cities Timnah and Ekron were within their territory. This must have caused some conflicts, as can be seen
from Judges 14–16. The discrepancy in the location of the
maḥănê-dān in the Book of Judges may indicate that the

[10] Astour, "Yahweh in Egyptian Topographical Lists," 17ff. Görg,
"Thutmosis III und die *šꜣsw* Region," 199ff.; M. Weippert, "Die Nomaden-
quelle: Ein Beitrag zur Topographie der Biqaᶜ im 2. Jahrtausend v. Chr.,"
in *Archäologie und Altes Testament: Festschrift K. Galling* (Tübingen, 1970) 264f.
Giveon also has noted that Shasu were to be found in Syria and northern
Palestine (*Les bédouins*, 267). Papyrus Anastasi I, 23:6–8 mentions Shasu as
marauding "bandits" in the Megiddo area.

[11] Astour, "Yahweh in Egyptian Topographical Lists," 30, n. 71.

Danites were not able to gain a secure foothold in this part of the country. In Judg 13:25, the Danite camp is located between Zorah and Eshtaol, but in 18:12, it is located closer to Kiriath-jearim, west of the city. The change of position could also indicate that the tribe had a relatively short stay in the area due to conflicts with the Philistines and pressure from the "Amorites" and Josephites (Judg 1:34ff.). These conflicts allegedly led the Danites to move north to Galilee and take the city of Leshem (Laish) which they renamed Dan (Judges 18).[12] This story[13] may have been based on old traditions about the upheavals and migrations of the 13th–12th centuries B.C. If we add to this the information in Judg 18:1 that the Danites had "no inheritance in Israel," we can perhaps conclude that they originally were strangers to the country. As mentioned in chap. 2, Y. Yadin has seen the Danites to be part of the Sea Peoples and identifies them with the Denyen who participated in the assault on Egypt.[14] This could mean that they were identical with the Danaoi mentioned in Greek texts[15] and the Danuna of the Amarna Texts (EA 151:52). According to Greek tradition, the ancestral father of the Danaoi was Danaos, son of Belos (i.e., the Babylonian Bel), and brother of Aegyptos. This may show that the Danaoi originally were Orientals.[16] Greek traditions dealing with the Danaoi connect Mopsos, the ruler of Colophon in Asia Minor, with the city of Ashkelon, where he is supposed to have died. They also mention the hero

[12] It is possible that the list of Danite cities in Josh 19:40–46 documents a later period, indicating that some Danites stayed in the South. See the discussion by A. Alt, "Judas Gaue unter Josia," *Palästinajahrbuch* 21 (1925) 100–116 (= *KS* II [Munich, 1953] 276ff.); and Aharoni, *The Land of the Bible*, 300.

[13] A. Malamat has compared the narrative of the Danites' move north with the Israelites' entrance into Canaan ("The Danite Migration and the Pan-Israelite Exodus-Conquest: A Biblical Narrative Pattern," *Biblica* 51 [1970] 1–16).

[14] Yadin, "And Dan, Why Did He Remain in Ships?" 9ff.

[15] Cf. M. Astour, *Hellenosemitica* (Leiden, 1967) 45–67.

[16] R. D. Barnett places the arrival of the Danuna in Syria ca. 1395 B.C., maintaining that "perhaps at this time they became known as invaders in Greece" ("Mopsos," *The Journal of Hellenic Studies* 73 [1953] 143).

Perseus, who is said to have freed Andromeda at Joppa.[17] Mopsos is also the name of the dynastic house of Azitawadda, king of the Danuna, as mentioned in the Karetepe inscription (8th century B.C.).[18] Another inscription from the same geographical area, that of Kilamuwa at Zincirli (9th century B.C.), lists the king of the Danuna as one of the king's enemies.[19]

It is possible that the Danites were part of a larger wave of peoples who migrated from Anatolia and Syria in various directions, and that they moved south to the coastal area of southern Palestine. The subsequent move to the northern part of Palestine could have occurred sometime after the Philistines had secured their position of power in the coastal area. The characterization of Dan in Deut 33:22 as a lion's cub leaping forth from Bashan considers northern Palestine to be their home territory.

P. C. Craigie has concluded that the Danites had nothing to do with the sea on the basis of his proposed meaning for the word $^{\jmath}nywt$ in the Danite saying in Judg 5:17.[20] Rejecting the usual translation 'ships,' he thinks that the term should be connected with Ugaritic $^{\jmath}an$, 'be at ease, relax.' Grammatically, however, his translation would need a *b* before $^{\jmath}nywt$ to be acceptable. The verse parallelism also makes the meaning 'ships' more probable. Three tribes are prevented from taking part in the battle because of connections with water: Gilead on the east side of the Jordan, Dan beside or under the protection of the Phoenicians (as were the former inhabitants of Laish), and Asher on the coast at their "landings." Hebrew *mprṣ* may mean 'landing' or 'bay, harbor'

---

[17] Cf. J. P. Brown, "Kothar, Kinyras, and Kythereia," *JSS* 10 (1965) 211ff.; N. K. Sandars, *The Sea Peoples* (London, 1978) 163f.; de Vaux, *The Early History of Israel*, 510.

[18] *KAI*, text 26. Cf. F. Bron, *Recherches sur les inscriptions phéniciennes de Karatepe* (Haute Études Orientales 11; Geneva, 1979) 12ff. For the spread of the name Mopsos, see Bron, *Recherches sur les inscriptions phéniciennes de Karatepe*, 172–76.

[19] *KAI*, text 24:7. Cf. F. M. Fales, "Kilamuwa and the Foreign Kings: Propaganda vs. Power," *Die Welt des Orients* 10 (1979) 6–22.

[20] P. C. Craigie, *Ugarit and the Old Testament* (Grand Rapids, 1983) 84f.

(cf. Arabic *furḍat*,[21] 'harbor'). In this case, v 17 would support the translation 'ships' for *ᵓnywt*.

Given this background, it is understandable why the poet in Judges 5 asks, "And Dan, why did he live close to the ships?" (v 17).[22] At the time of the battle described in Judges 5, the Danites may have been Sea Peoples or Phoenician dependents who were still not part of the Israelite community. Therefore, the tradition in Judges 17–18 may be seen as a later Danite claim to be Israelite, and an attempt to make their temple and priesthood part of a Yahwistic tradition. The biblical historian has turned the tradition against the Danites, however, by criticizing Dan's idol, temple, and levitical priesthood.[23]

The people and the district of Asher represent a group which originally was Canaanite and later became part of the nation of Israel. Even though the biblical genealogies have made them Israelites from the beginning, Gen 30:12–13 indicates that this was not the case. The name Asher, *i-ś-r*, is known from an inscription of Pharaoh Seti I (1291–1272),[24] and also from an inscription in the temple of Ramses II at Abydos.[25] It also appears in the Papyrus Anastasi I, 23:6, from the period of Ramses II. This text is a letter from an Egyptian scribe named Hori to another scribe, giving some insights into the geography of Syria-Palestine and its peoples from the roads he traveled. The scribe mentions a certain Qazardi who was the chief ruler of the people of Asher, *i-ś-rw*.[26] In all three instances the name is preceded by the

---

[21] See G. F. Moore, *Critical and Exegetical Commentary on Judges* (ICC; Edinburgh, 1895) 155ff.

[22] T. Dothan thinks that the Philistine pottery found at Tel Dan supports Yadin's thesis (*The Philistines and their Material Culture* [New Haven and London, 1982] 84).

[23] Cf. my *Aspects of Syncretism in Israelite Religion* (Lund, 1963) 26f. This deuteronomistic criticism should be compared with Ezekiel's denunciation in 44:10 of several Levites' service of idols.

[24] See J. Simons, *Handbook for the Study of Egyptian Topographical Lists Relating to Western Asia* (Leiden, 1937) 147, list 17:4.

[25] Simons, *Handbook for the Study of Egyptian Topographical Lists*, 162, list 25:8.

[26] Helck, *Die Beziehungen*, 280, n. 24.

determinative for land. The exact location of the land of Asher is not given, but in Papyrus Anastasi, it appears to be close to Megiddo.[27] The scribe appears to have met Qazardi after he had been at Megiddo and before he arrived at Joppa. This would indicate that the Asherites and their land should be located somewhere south of Megiddo, perhaps in the western foothills of central Palestine around Beth-Horon and Aijalon down to the Gezer area.[28]

The Asherite clans in this territory could perhaps have been the "Amorites" mentioned in Judg 1:35 who inhabited the geographical districts of Shaalbim, Aijalon, and Har-Heres (Beth-Shemesh).[29] Since much of this area later was considered Benjaminite territory, some of these clans came to be included in the Benjaminite genealogies, as indicated by 1 Chr 8:12. These Asherite clans may have been Canaanite clans which moved up from the coastal areas to the foothills of the central mountainous region. As time went on, they became affiliated with neighboring peoples and finally became part of the Benjaminites in biblical historiography.

The Asherites in the western Galilee in the Phoenician areas first became Israelites at the time of the kingdom of David. This accounts for Asher's status as the "son" of one of the handmaids in Gen 30:12 and not a son of Leah or Rachel. This is the way the tradition states that Asher was a latecomer into Israelite society. The same holds true for the peoples of Gad, Dan, and Naphtali. Originally they were all Canaanite peoples whose territories were incorporated into the nation of Israel under David, at the latest. The name

[27] The scribe went on to Joppa where he got into trouble because of a beautiful woman, losing his chariot and perhaps something else too. He was able to get a new chariot at the Egyptian base at Joppa.

[28] Heber, the son of Beriah is reported here to be an Asherite, cf. Gen 46:17, but in 1 Chr 8:12 he is the son of El-paal, a Benjaminite, brother to Beriah. Beriah is associated with Aijalon and a place Gath in 1 Chr 7:21ff. and 8:19. For the borders of Benjamin, see Josh 15:5–11, 18:11–20 and Aharoni, *The Land of the Bible*, 255ff., cf. also 244.

[29] Cf. Aharoni, *The Land of the Bible*, 236; Herrmann, *A History of Israel*, 93; and Diana Edelman, "The 'Ashurites' of Eshbaal's State (2 Sam 2:9)," *PEQ* 117 (1985) 85–91.

Israel therefore originally did not belong to these territories and their peoples.[30]

In light of what has been maintained so far, the central highlands were a place of refuge time and time again for new peoples who moved in and settled down.[31] Since the central highland area was called Kharu (Hurru) by the Egyptians, one would expect some of its regions to have been inhabited by Hurrians. It is noteworthy in this connection that the central city of the highlands, Shechem, is called in the MT text of Gen 34:2 the "son of Hamor, a Hivite," while several of the LXX manuscripts read Hurrite here rather than Hivite. The biblical writers seem to have experienced some confusion between the terms Hivite and Horite. In Gen 36:2, for instance, Zibeon is called a Hivite, but in v 20 he is counted as a Hurrian.[32] From this we may conclude that Shechem was considered to have been built by northerners and that part of the population in and around Shechem might have been part of the same stock for a

---

[30] S. Herrmann, among others, points out that "in essentials the Galilean tribes are the ones which are regarded as children of the maids, or has having been born later" (*A History of Israel*, 110, n. 57). Bright also acknowledges that the "Israel that emerged drew together within its structure groups of the most heterogeneous origin" (*A History of Israel*, 133).

[31] For the Bronze Age demographic picture, cf. Thompson, *The Settlement of Palestine in the Bronze Age*, 34; and the corrections given by Kay Prag, "Continuity and Migration in the South Levant in the Late Third Millennium: A Review of T. L. Thompson and some other Views," *PEQ* 116 (1984) 58–68. See also Sapin, "La géographie humaine de la Syrie-Palestine," 113–86.

[32] For Hivites and Hurrians, see for instance, Gibson, "Some Important Ethnic Terms in the Pentateuch," 229f.; A. Kuschke, "Hiwwiter in ha-ʿAi?," in *Wort und Geschichte: Festschrift für Karl Elliger* (ed. H. Gese and H. P. Rüger; AOAT 18; Neukirchen-Vluyn, 1973) 115–19; M. Görg, "Hiwwiter im 13. Jahrhundert v. Chr.," *Ugarit Forschungen* 8 (1976) 53ff. I. M. Diakonoff thinks that the Hurrians could have brought the Kur-Araxes culture "in the form of the Khirbet Kerak culture to southern Syria and Palestine" ("Evidence on the Ethnic Divisions of the Hurrians," *Studies on the Civilization and Culture of Nuzi and the Hurrians in Honor of Ernest R. Lacheman* [ed. M. A. Morrison and D. I. Owen; Winona Lake, IN, 1981] 88ff.).

long time. If we look at the names of some of the city
rulers of the Amarna period, like Labayu of Shechem,
Shuwardata of Gath, and Abdi-Hepa of Jerusalem, it is clear
that parts of Palestine were ruled by non-Canaanite peoples.
Again, Amenhotep II's list of prisoners of war from his
second Syro-Palestinian campaign shows that around thirty
percent of them were Hurrians, and this explains why the
country could be called Kharu.[33]
    There are traditions about the peoples in the Shechem
area having associated themselves with different clans which
settled in the vicinity. In the Hebrew Bible, the association
entered into is expressed with the term *běrît*, 'covenant,
treaty,' Josh 8:33ff.; 24:1ff.; Gen 35:1; cf. Deut 7:2. The
Amarna correspondence also mentions that the Shechemites
joined a group of people who were hostile to the prince of
Jerusalem. In EA 287:30f. and 289:20ff. Abdi-Hepa of Jerusalem accuses the sons of Labayu of having given the land of
Shechem over to the *ᶜapīru*.[34] This probably reflects the
making of a *běrît* between the rulers of Shechem and the
ᶜapīru people. H. Reviv concludes from EA 271:9ff. and
273:15ff. that the *ᶜapīru* were hired to assist in the expansion
of Shechem's borders, "a practice used later by Abimelech,
who is said to have hired 'empty (worthless) and reckless
men,'" (Judg 9:4,[35] cf. 11:3). This may indicate that Shechem
was still the center of a political unit. How large it was is not
known. The Shechem area could have been inhabited in the
time of Gideon and Abimelech by descendants of the *ᶜapīru*
hired by Labayu and his sons. The archaeological survey
mentioned in chap. 3[36] shows that several new sites had
been settled after ca. 1450 B.C.[37] Many of these settlements
may have been built during Labayu's rule. His territorial
expansions[38] both north and south from the central city of

---

[33] See above, p. 12 and cf. Bright, *A History of Israel*, 116.

[34] Cf. *ANET*, 489.

[35] H. Reviv, "The Government of Shechem in the el-Amarna Period
and the Days of Abimelech," *IEJ* 16 (1966) 253.

[36] Cf. pp. 25f.

[37] Campbell, "The Shechem Area Survey," 41.

[38] Labayu's kingdom is not an ordinary city-state in the sense of a city
with its immediate surroundings. In the 14th century, Shechem included

Shechem may have encouraged people to settle in the Shechem plain (fig. 2). Abdi-Hepa could have labeled these new settlers ʿapīru. No traces of a material culture which indicate that a new ethnic group entered the area have been reported.[39]

The lack of stratigraphic break in the transitional period between the Late Bronze and Early Iron I periods at Tell Balaṭa, ancient Shechem,[40] strengthens the argument that there was no military invasion and conquest on a grand scale.[41] As has been pointed out, the material culture at Shechem does not show any new or non-Canaanite features which can be associated with a new group of people. The Hebrew Bible and archaeological evidence agree that no conquest occurred at Shechem in the transitional Late Bronze–Iron I period. The city was destroyed later during the Early Iron I period. This destruction has been associated with King Abimelech's sacking of Shechem, reported in Judges 9.[42] Shechem is one of the few instances where the textual and archaeological material seems to give the same picture for this transitional time.

What we see here, then, is that the Hurrians, ʿapīru, and others settled in the areas around Shechem. As settled peoples, they could have been known as Israelites, i.e., peoples living in the territory called Israel.

The complaint in Judg 8:33 that the "people of Israel" made Baal-Berith of Shechem their god shows that the religion of the Israelites was the normal "Canaanite" form of

---

most of the central hill country North of Jerusalem to the Jezreel Valley (cf. Helck, *Die Beziehungen*, 188; Aharoni, *The Land of the Bible*, 175; and de Vaux, *Early History of Israel*, 801). Labayu could be seen as a predecessor to Saul.

[39] We do not know whether these settlements were used temporarily or year round.

[40] G. E. Wright, *Shechem: The Biography of a City* (New York and Toronto, 1965) 78.

[41] Khirbet er-Rabud is another site which has no destruction layer from this period, see M. Kochavi, "Khirbet Rabud = Debir," *Tel Aviv* 1 (1974) 2ff. K. Galling already identified Debir with Khirbet Rabud in the 1950s ("Zur Lokalisierung von Debir," *ZDPV* 70 [1954] 135ff.).

[42] Cf. E. F. Campbell, J. F. Ross, and L. E. Toombs, "The Eighth Campaign at Balaṭah (Shechem)," *BASOR* 204 (1971) 2–17, esp. 15.

1. Shechem
2. Jerusalem
3. Bethlehem

30 miles

Fig. 2. The probable extension of the kingdoms of Shechem and Jerusalem.

religion that was practiced in the Shechemite territory. Similarly, Gideon's ephod idol in Ophrah, which is castigated in Judg 8:24–27,[43] preserves a glimpse of the kind of religious practices found in the territory of Israel prior to the artificial retrojection of monotheistic Yahwism from the narrator's later time frame into this period. We also learn that Ophrah was Gideon's seat of residence, which would mean that Gideon probably had become the ruler of Shechem through a *bĕrît*, as H. Reviv has maintained.[44] Whether this Ophrah is identical with the city of Micah in Judges 17 is not known, but it is possible.[45] Both Micah and Gideon are said to have made an ephod of jewelry. This may say something about their social status.

It is not known how long the Shechemite kingdom existed, but biblical tradition suggests that it continued for quite some time. Both Gideon, who is said to have resembled a king (Judg 8:18), and Abimelech, who had the title of king (Judg 9:6), were rulers of the territory of Shechem. The extent of the political kingdom they controlled is not indicated. It is possible that the kingdom disintegrated at Abimelech's death who had sacked the capital city, Shechem. Philistine rule may also have been a contributing factor in its demise. In any event, Shechem was no more than an insignificant village from the Early Iron I period down to the time of Jeroboam I.

When Saul created a nation in the hill country, the inhabitants of the Shechem area may have welcomed it because, like most other peoples in the mountains, they saw Saul as a leader against Philistine oppression. It is probable, therefore, that the Hebrews who were rallying to Saul's banner (1 Sam 14:21) included the people of the former kingdom of Abimelech. The wars of Gideon and Abimelech may be seen as attempts to unite some of the peoples of the

---

[43] Cf. my *Aspects of Syncretism*, 14ff.

[44] Reviv, "The Government of Shechem," 253, n. 5.

[45] Y. Aharoni likes to identify Ophrah with modern ʿAffuleh, but Gideon's rulership was not acknowledged north of the Jezreel valley (*The Land of the Bible*, 263).

hills[46] into a political unit such as had existed in the days of Labayu. Saul was the first person to succeed in making the territory of Israel into a nation and David rebuilt and expanded it.

The Gibeonites are another group which the biblical tradition considers to have been foreigners who settled in the hills. Although it is not known when they moved up to the highlands, circumstantial evidence allows us to propose that they arrived in the latter part of the Late Bronze period. Excavations at Tell el-Jib, which has been identified with Gibeon, have uncovered some LB II tombs and a city wall, 3.2 to 3.4 m. wide, which is thought to date from the Early Iron I period.[47] It would have taken some time for the new settlers to have been able to build fortified cities and create the Gibeonite city federation of Gibeon, Chephirah, Beeroth, and Kiriath-jearim (cf. Josh 9:17). The massive wall at el-Jib may be a material indication of the beginning of the political role of the Gibeonite cities.

According to Josh 9:7, the Gibeonites were of Edomite-Hurrian or Hivite (Cilician) ancestry.[48] In 1 Chr 8:29 a certain Jeiel is called the "father of Gibeon," and in 9:35 he also is mentioned as the ancestral father of king Saul.[49] Since Jeiel's wife was named Maacah, which is known to be an Aramean name, we could perhaps maintain that the Gibeonites mingled with some Aramean group which also had settled in the hills. In order to emphasize their "non-

---

[46] Cf. B. Otzen, *Israeliterne i Palaestina: Det Gamle Israels historie, religion og kultur* (Copenhagen, 1977) 128.

[47] J. B. Pritchard, "Gibeon's History in the Light of Excavation," (VTSup 7; Leiden, 1960) 1ff.; "A Bronze Age Necropolis at Gibeon," *BA* 24 (1961) 22f.

[48] Cf., for instance, J. M. Grintz, "The Treaty of Joshua with the Gibeonites," *JAOS* 86 (1966) 121, n. 39 and the citations above in n. 32.

[49] J. Blenkinsopp has investigated the lists of Gibeonite and Saulidic names and has concluded that there is "an interesting overlap with names in Edom and in the region south of Judah" (*Gibeon and Israel* [Society for Old Testament Study, Monograph Series 2; Cambridge, 1972] 26). Saul's name and possibly also Kish's were known in early Edom (Blenkinsopp, *Gibeon and Israel*, 59f.). See also A. Demsky, "The Genealogy of Gibeon (I Chronicles 9:35-44): Biblical and Epigraphic Considerations," *BASOR* 202 (1971) 16ff.

Israelite" origin, the writer of 2 Sam 21:2 labels them Amorites.

Josh 9:3ff. reports that at some point in time, the Gibeonites became associated by treaty with the peoples of the hills, the Israelites. This text seems to refer to an event which created a conflict between the two treaty partners, since it is said to have been made under false pretence.[50] As a result, the Gibeonites are said to have been punished and to have been made temple servants of low status. But the question is, what temple? The reference to the temple clearly shows that the text is late, and points to either a late pre-exilic time or to the post-exilic period.

There could, naturally, have been several conflicts between the Gibeonites and their neighbors over the course of time. As to the treaty between Joshua and the Gibeonites, it is impossible to establish its historicity and the truth entirely escapes us. The narrator may have used old traditions about conflicts between the Gibeonites and their neighbors, but from his Jerusalemite ideological horizon, he has used both the Gibeonites and Saul as foils within his pro-Davidic historiography.[51] The narrator may have known about some form of feud between Saul and the Gibeonites, because in 2 Sam 21:5 the men of Gibeon say that Saul wanted to exterminate them. There evidently was a break between Saul and the Gibeonites, but its cause is not preserved.[52] We must be wary of drawing firm conclusions about the scope of the conflict because a centuries-long anti-Saulidic attitude

[50] This treaty cannot be interpreted to represent a "general process of defection by indigenous peoples from their aristocratic overlords" as B. Halpern has done ("Gibeon: Israelite Diplomacy in the Conquest Era," *CBQ* 37 [1975] 312). The Gibeonites did not have any Canaanite overlords.

[51] For Joshua as a leading figure in Benjaminite traditions, see Herrmann, *A History of Israel*, 97. Is it possible that Saul has been used as a model to paint the picture of Joshua? For a list of points of contact between the two figures, see S. Cook, *Critical Notes on Old Testament History* (London, 1907) 21, 28, 144.

[52] J. Blenkinsopp thinks that the men of Gibeon finally rejected Saul, just as the elders of Shechem who accepted Abimelech at first later rejected him (*Gibeon and Israel*, 38). S. Yeivin assumes that there was an old feud between Saul's ancestors and the Gibeonites ("The Benjaminite Settlement in the Western Part of their Territory," *IEJ* 21 [1971] 154).

within the Davidic court could have led to an exaggeration of the facts.

Josh 9:6ff. may be an attempt in later times to explain the status of the former inhabitants of the Gibeonite enclave, which has set the hatred of this "foreign" group back into the pre-monarchic period. Some of the content and phrasing in the story in Joshua 9 indicate a late date of composition and tend to suggest that an old treaty tradition has been reworked to the detriment of the Gibeonites. The Gibeonites' claim that they have heard about all that Yahweh had done in Egypt reflects the Exodus wonders which, as maintained above, is part of the late historiography of the Hebrew Bible. This motif is part of a certain literary activity during the exilic and post-exilic periods when people pondered the cause of the catastrophe of 586 B.C. and needed a reason and proof for their right to the land. The statement in v 27 that the Gibeonites were made "hewers of wood and drawers of water"[53] (i.e., a humiliating and womanly job)[54] for the temple has nothing to do with "invading" or pre-monarchic Israelites.[55] The story is an etiology.[56]

In addition, as J. Wellhausen, among others, has pointed out,[57] it is not Joshua who conducts the negotiations with the Gibeonites in Josh 9:7, 14, but the "men of Israel" who act on behalf of the people. This could show either that we are dealing with a second, later source, as Wellhausen

[53] According to Deut 29:10, these hewers and drawers were *gērîm*, 'strangers in the midst of the camp.'

[54] Cf. D. J. A. Clines, "KRT 111–114 (iii:7–10): 'Gatherers of Wood and Drawers of Water,'" *UF* 8 (1976) 23–26.

[55] J. Liver has pointed out that the "speeches of the Gibeonites (*vv.* 9–10, 24–5) . . . are similar in outlook to the Book of Deuteronomy," but still thinks that the composition is from the time of Saul ("The Literary History of Joshua IX," *JSS* 8 [1963] 229f., 243).

[56] We should note in this connection a statement from A. G. Auld: "Much of the material under review is not raw source-data for the modern historian, but rather the solutions and deductions of his counterparts in the later biblical period—of quite as much interest, of course, once recognized for what they are" (*Joshua, Moses and the Land* [Edinburgh, 1980] 110).

[57] J. Wellhausen, *Prolegomena to the History of Ancient Israel* (reprinted, Cleveland, 1957) 356f.

suggested, or that the narrator slipped in his reconstruction of the acts of the great conqueror of the land and told something which comes closer to the truth, perhaps reflecting the problems which the post-exilic community encountered with its neighbors.

Verse 15, on the other hand, preserves an important detail in its report that the Israelites took the oath and swore. In ancient Near Eastern treaty rituals, it usually was the subordinate party, the vassal, who took the oath.[58] This makes one suspect that the etiology in Joshua 9 may be a late adaptation of some older event which has made the originally inferior group into the superior one. The historical event lying behind this tradition could have been a treaty between Saul, representing Benjamin, and the Gibeonite city federation, which made the Gibeonites the more powerful and well-organized part of the new kingdom.[59] The Gibeonite enclave could have been one of the earliest parts of Saul's kingdom, if K. D. Schunk is right that it served as Saul's first capital.[60] Were the Gibeonites perhaps opposed to Saul's other expansions because they lost their position as a powerful ally and were sidestepped as Saul's territory grew? The conflict that arose may have forced Saul to treat the Gibeonites harshly, and may have necessitated moving his residence to a new site, Saul's Gibeah.[61]

Combining the indication for a reworking of an early, possibly Saulide treaty tradition with the occurrence of the

[58] Cf. D. J. McCarthy, *Treaty and Covenant* (Rome, 1963) 46f.; Blenkinsopp, *Gibeon and Israel*, 40.

[59] For a suggestion that the treaty was concluded with early Benjaminites at the end of the Amarna Age, see Blenkinsopp, *Gibeon and Israel*, 35–39.

[60] K. D. Schunk, *Benjamin: Untersuchungen zur Entstehung und Geschichte eines israelitischen Stammes* (BZAW 86; Berlin, 1963) 132f.; Blenkinsopp, *Gibeon and Israel*, 64. In addition, see my discussion about Gibeon and Saul's *dwd* (1 Sam 10:14ff.) in *Royal Administration and National Religion in Ancient Palestine*, 21. I. Hylander thought that Saul had intended to make Gibeon his capital (*Der literarische Samuel-Saul-Komplex (1. Sam. 1–15)* [Uppsala and Leipzig, 1932] 262, 265).

[61] There is a possible connection between Josh 9:3ff. and 2 Samuel 21. David's sacrifice of the sons of Saul to appease the Gibeonites resulted in the making of a "new" treaty. The descendants of Saul replaced the

etiological explanation of the Gibeonites' status as temple laborers and the use of the late Exodus motif, it seems that Joshua 9 in its present form is largely a fictitious creation, probably of the post-exilic community. The returnees from Babylonia did not want to have anything to do with the peoples of the land, not even with the Judahites who had never been exiled. This attitude could have led them to denigrate in their historiography the surrounding peoples they found when they returned. This may explain why the Gibeonites became "hewers of wood and drawers of water" (i.e., menial workers at the temple), a condition which was then retrojected back into the days of Joshua (the idealized champion of holy-war ideology who eliminated foreign peoples from the land) through the adaptation of a Saulide-Gibeonite treaty tradition. Their status as servile laborers in the post-exilic community allowed them to live in peace with the new society in Judah.[62]

In addition to archaeological remains, any reconstruction of the history of the central hill country for the period between Merneptah's mention of Israel and the emergence of the Israelite kingdom under Saul must take into consideration the biblical textual material. While it is rich in information, it must be analyzed carefully to sort historical data from theological fiction, since the Bible is a product of faith which represents theological reflections of later periods about earlier events. The purpose of the texts is not primarily to present the historical sequence of events.[63]

---

sacrificial animal in a treaty ceremony. The transfer of the ark of Yahweh from Kiriath-jearim to Jerusalem probably should be seen against this background. When the relationship between the Gibeonites and the new Israelite monarchy was restored, Yahweh became the kingdom's main god again. As such, he had to be moved to the new capital, Jerusalem. See my article, "The Travels of the Ark," *JNES* 43 (1984) 141–49.

[62] The great pool and water tunnel at Gibeon probably contributed to the appellation of the Gibeonites as "drawers of water." For the probability that Gibeon was settled during the early Persian period, see E. Stern, *Material Culture of the Land of the Bible in the Persian Period 538–332 B.C.* (Warminster, 1982) 32ff.

[63] J. M. Sasson, for instance, has noted that "it might be possible to regard the folkloristic materials preserved in Genesis–Judges (e.g., the

The Book of Judges, for instance, presents an ideological reconstruction of the pre-monarchic period which is concerned mainly with events in the northern parts of the central highlands. The descriptions of events are structured according to a determined literary pattern[64] which unfortunately only preserves small tidbits of actual history. The pattern used is one of recurring change from an ideal, orderly epoch to an evil, chaotic one. It has the following main stages:

1. A right leader and a right Yahwistic cult; when the leader dies,
2. the people abandon Yahweh and turn to the gods of Canaan.
3. Yahweh punishes the people by subjecting them to their neighbors.
4. The people of "Israel" cry to Yahweh for help.
5. Yahweh answers them by raising up a "savior," sometimes called a "judge."
6. He delivers the people from oppression, and peace enters the stage for forty years.
7. The "judge" dies, and the cycle starts over again.

Such a pattern of religious advocacy is of little use in reconstructing history.[65] All that can be termed historical

---

saga of the Patriarchs, the escape from Egypt, the conquest of the land) as the work of intellectuals, who beginning with the second half of the Monarchic period, sought to present a defeated and fragmented nation edifying models worthy of imitation" (*Ruth, A New Translation with a Philological Commentary and a Formalistic–Folkloristic Interpretation* [The Johns Hopkins Near Eastern Studies; Baltimore and London, 1979] 250).

[64] In Judges 17–21, the so-called "appendices" to the Book of Judges, this pattern had no function to fill.

[65] This is an old Near Eastern stylistic pattern. See, among others, T. E. Peet, *A Comparative Study of the Literatures of Egypt, Palestine and Mesopotamia* (London, 1931) 120f.; H. G. Güterbock, "Die historische Tradition und ihre literarische Gestaltung bei Babyloniern und Hethitern," *ZA* 42 (1934) 15ff. This pattern of change is also found in the so-called "Akkadian Weidner Chronicle," a propagandistic text which classifies kings into a good or evil category. For the text, see A. K. Grayson, *Assyrian and Babylonian Chronicles* (Texts from Cuneiform Sources 5; Locust Valley, NY, 1975) 43, 145ff. The idea of alternations between orderly and chaotic

information is perhaps the occurrence of some conflicts between groups of people and the names of the individuals, clans, and possible rulers who played a leading role in the events described. The so-called "judges" or "saviors" probably were petty rulers in the hills whose names were remembered long after their deaths.[66] The biblical historiographer has given these rulers and chieftains the status of leaders over all the Israelites, i.e., the inhabitants of the central hills. In this way he has endeavored to construct a nation of Israel before it actually existed. At the same time, he has created a chronological sequence out of these stories.[67]

The appearance of the *mal ʾak yahweh*, 'angel (or, messenger) of Yahweh,' in Judg 5:23 as the leader of Israel tends to show that the narratives of the conquest and the Judges were composed at a late date. The *mal ʾāk* occurs elsewhere in Exod 23:20 and 33:2 as the leader of Israel who is about to be sent to lead the people into Canaan and liquidate the Amorites, Hittites, Perizzites, Canaanites, Hivites, and Jebusites. He occurs again in Judg 2:1 as the one who leads the

---

periods occurs in some Akkadian and Egyptian "prophecies," see H. Hunger and S. A. Kaufman, "A New Akkadian Prophecy Text," *JAOS* 95 (1975) 371–75; R. D. Biggs, "More Babylonian Prophecies," *Iraq* 29 (1967) 117f.; and W. Helck, *Die Prophezeihung des Nfr.tj* (Kleine Ägyptische Texte; Wiesbaden, 1970).

[66] The classification into "major" and "minor" judges is no more than a scholarly-theological invention inspired by Max Weber's theory about "charismatic" leaders, which he thought to be the real judges (*Gesammelte Aufsätze zur Religionssoziologie*, III: *Das antike Judentum* [Tübingen, 1921] 92–95). See also Judg 2:17 which mentions judges of no "Yahwistic" importance.

[67] Judg 1:21 and 20:1–18 indicate that the Book of Judges is written from a Judahistic point of view. Chap. 1 also shows another conquest tradition than the one in the Book of Joshua which would speak for different origins of these traditions. The above-mentioned literary pattern of change is certainly the work of one author. Cf. also D. W. Gooding, who advocates that the Book of Judges "was the work of one mind which saw the significance of the history recorded in the sources, perceived the trends it exhibited and carefully selected and positioned each piece of source material so that the symmetrical structure of the whole would make those trends apparent to the reader" ("The Composition of the Book of Judges," *Eretz Israel* [Harry M. Orlinsky Volume] 16 [1982] 77).

people from Gilgal to Bochim. These verses show a programmatic tendency to underscore the divine involvement in and approval of the right of Israel to the promised land.[68] The statement that the peoples of Canaan who are listed should be blotted out or annihilated puts this angelic motif in the post-exilic period.[69]

We do not need to go too deeply into the well-known details about the judges. Shamgar ben Anath has been remembered because of his battle with the Philistines. Note that his name may be Hurrian-Canaanite, and that the phrase "ben Anath" characterizes him as a man of royalty, i.e., the "son" of his goddess Anath[70] (Judg 3:31). Abdon is said to be from the Amalakite city of Pirathon in Ephraim (Judg 12:13–15) and thus may have been an Amalekite himself. Elon probably ruled over just the territory of Zebulon (Judg 12:11f.). Similarly, Tola ben Puah ben Dodo probably ruled over Issachar (Judg 10:1–2).[71] Jair and Jephthah are clearly Transjordanian chieftains (Judg 10:3; 11:1ff.). Gideon-Jerubbaal may have ruled over a larger territory than most of the others. It included parts of the old Shechem kingdom, but its full extent has not been preserved in tradition.[72] Samson is the most legendary figure of the

68 J. Van Seters notes that in Exod 23:20ff., the "angel of Yahweh" is to be seen as "a guiding and directing force but is never actually present as a person" (*In Search of History* [New Haven and London, 1983] 341). This would indicate a post-exilic intellectualism.

69 M. Noth saw Exod 23:20–33 as an addition with a "deuteronomistic stamp in style and content." The promise of the land from Egypt to the Euphrates is a reference to the Davidic kingdom (*Exodus* [OT Library; Philadelphia, 1962] 193).

70 The term "son" is usually part of a legitimation claim by a king. Cf. also A. Vincent, *La religion des judéo-araméens d'Elephantine* (Paris, 1937) 643. For royalty as "sons" and "daughters" of a deity, see also O. Eissfeldt, "Gottesnamen in Personennamen als Symbole menschlicher Qualitäten," *Festschrift Walter Baetke* (ed. K. Rudolph, R. Heller, and E. Walter; Weimar, 1966) 110–17.

71 Tola's name could be the same kind as Shamgar's. Cf. G. Buccellati, who states that "the rulers regularly added to their names the name(s) of their father and sometimes their grandfather" (*Cities and Nations of Ancient Syria* [Studi Semitici 26; Rome, 1967] 168).

72 Since Gideon is described as a king's son, he must have been of royal birth. The claim that he turned down the offer of kingship is

group. He never appears as a chief of any part of the country—even though he might have been one (Judges 13–16).[73]

The priest Eli of Shiloh is not considered a judge by the Book of Judges. Nevertheless, he is said to have been judging (i.e., ruling)[74] Israel for forty years, one generation (1 Sam 4:18). He has been made the last leader before Samuel. His political role, if any, escapes us. In its present form, the narrative in 1 Samuel 1–4 contrasts Eli and his Canaanite priesthood with Samuel and the Zadokites. The biblical narrator states bluntly that "the word of Yahweh was rare in those days" (1 Sam 3:1), thus betraying his recognition that Yahweh was not yet the god of the whole country. Eli's name may indicate that he was not a priest of Yahweh but rather a priest of the god ᶜly.[75]

Micah, whose story is told in Judges 17–18, was certainly more than a wealthy farmer, as he often has been described. The biblical writer has not characterized him as a judge in Israel, probably because he fought one of the tribes, the

---

probably the narrator's way of saving his "theocratic" ideal. We should note that his son Abimelech also has the title, king. For the problem of the double name, Gideon-Jerubbaal, consult J. A. Emerton, "Gideon and Jerubbaal," *JTS* n.s. 27 (1976) 289–312. Jerubbaal can be seen as a regnal name of King Gideon. A. Neher sees the narrative about Gideon and his family to be a blueprint for kingship (*L'essence du prophétisme* [Paris, 1955] 199).

[73] R. Mayer-Opificius maintains that the depiction of Samson as a hero is one of the "*sechs- oder achtlockigen Helden*" of the period of Sargon II ("Simson, der sechslockige Held?" *UF* 14 [1982] 149–51).

[74] For the Semitic term *špṭ*, see among others, H. W. Hertzberg, "Die Entwicklung des Begriffes מִשְׁפָּט im Alten Testament," *ZAW* 40 (1922) 256ff.; A. Marzal, "The Provincial Governor at Mari: His Title and Appointment," *JNES* 30 (1971) 188–217; W. Richter, "Zu den 'Richtern Israels,'" *ZAW* 77 (1965) 60f.; M. Stol, "Akkadisches *šapiṭum šapaṭum* und westsemitisches *špṭ*," *Bibliotheca Orientalis* 29 (1972) 276–77; Ahlström, *Aspects of Syncretism in Israelite Religion*, 19; and K. W. Whitelam, *The Just King: Monarchical Judicial Authority in Ancient Israel* (JSOT Suppl. Ser. 12; Sheffield, 1979) 46–69.

[75] See among others, H. S. Nyberg, *Studien zum Hoseabuche* (UUÅ 1935:6; Uppsala, 1935) 58ff.; M. Pope, in *Wörterbuch der Mythologie* I (Stuttgart, 1965) 255; M. Dahood, *Psalms* I (Anchor Bible 16; Garden City, NY, 1966) 117.

Danites. His status as a prince or petty ruler, however, can be deduced from his mother's allocation of money to him to build an idol, his building of a temple (*bêt* *ʾĕlôhîm*), and his installation of one of his sons as priest (17:3–5). The latter two actions were royal prerogatives. He is also said to have pursued the migrating Danites who had robbed him of his idol and had taken his new priest, a Levite, whom he apparently employed after his son.[76] No farmer could have had an army strong enough to consider waging war against a migrating people. Micah is also said to have resided at Ophrah, but it is not known whether he was a ruler there before or after Gideon.[77]

Samuel is another local ruler from the hills of Ephraim who has been raised to the position of the last judge and has been made the transitional figure between the periods of the judges and the monarchy. He has been made a ruler of all the Israelites, and seems to be one of the deuteronomist's ideal leaders. He is depicted as a leader of a theocracy in the modern sense of the term—an idea which was completely foreign to 11th century peoples of the Near East. The ancient theocracy was the nation which was divinely ruled through the god's viceroy, the king.[78] For the biblical writer, Samuel inaugurates a new epoch, the monarchic era. One may doubt, however, that Samuel played as important a role as the biblical narrator has assigned him; indeed, sometimes

[76] Micah's mother has been described in terms of a *gĕbīrāh*, the mighty lady, "queen mother," who had her own administration and wealth. The biblical narrator has preserved some important facts here, even though he has avoided depicting Micah as the true ruler he was because it did not fit his historiographic pattern. J. Morgenstern sees Micah as a local chief, the "head of a settlement" ("The Ark, the Ephod, and the 'Tent of Meeting,'" *HUCA* 18 [1944] 4). R. G. Boling labels Micah a "cultic opportunist" (*Judges* [Anchor Bible 6A; Garden City, NY, 1975] 255). Originally, the text probably was intended to legitimate the Danites as Israelites, but the deuteronomist has turned the end of the story against them (Judg 18:31). Cf. my *Aspects of Syncretism*, 25f.

[77] R. T. O'Callaghan dates Gideon to ca. 1070 B.C., which would have made him a contemporary of Hadad of Edom in Gen 36:39 (*Aram Naharaim* [Rome, 1948] 121, n. 3).

[78] See Ahlström, *Royal Administration and National Religion in Ancient Palestine*, 1ff.

he looks too much like a Moses. Fortunately, 1 Sam 7:15ff. seems to preserve the territory which Samuel actually controlled. He is reported to have had his residence in Ramah and to have gone on an annual circuit to Mizpah, Gilgal, and Bethel, thus renewing the bonds with Yahweh and his people at these sanctuaries. So then, these cities and their surrounding areas may have constituted the territory which Samuel governed (*špṭ*).

The poem in Judges 5, the so-called "Song of Deborah," is the one biblical text which has been used most often as the basis for a historical reconstruction of the political situation before ca. 1100 B.C.[79] The text's orthography is usually cited to defend such an early date. This in itself, however, does not prove the poem's age since poetry often utilizes archaic forms and patterns.[80] Instead, the text does not appear to date from the same time as the battle it commemorates. The phrase in v 6, "In the days of Shamgar ben Anath, in the days of Jael . . ." shows that the poet is referring to events of a distant past.[81] Neither does the poem accurately record the existence of a ten-tribe league or an all-Israelite battle against Sisera and his army. Judg 5:18 (along with 4:6, 10) states that only Zebulon and Naphtali risked their lives on the battlefield.[82] The account appears to have been based on

[79] K. Budde was one of the earlier persons to date the text to ca. 1100 B.C. (*Geschichte der althebräischen Literatur* [Leipzig, 1906] 7).

[80] Compare for instance, B. Alster's statement that "the narrative patterns in 'classical' Sumerian myths, epics, and folktales are nearly universal, and they do not basically differ from those observed in e.g. Russian folktales" ("Early Patterns in Sumerian Literature," in *Kramer Anniversary Volume* [ed. B. Eichler, with the assistance of J. W. Heimerdinger and Å. W. Sjöberg; AOAT 25; Neukirchen-Vluyn, 1976] 14). With this in mind, we could perhaps suspect that poetic patterns and expressions remained unchanged for centuries in ancient Palestine also.

[81] A. D. H. Mayes dates the poem to the end of the period of the Judges ("The Historical Context of the Battle against Sisera," *VT* 19 [1969] 359). Cf. also P. R. Ackroyd, "The Composition of the Song of Deborah," *VT* 2 (1952) 162; Ahlström, "Judges 5:20f. and History," 288. J. Halévy sees Jael in Judg 5:6 as being the wife of Shamgar ben Anath and, thus, not identical with Jael of v 24 (*Recherches biblique: L'histoire des origines d'après la Genèse* II [Paris, 1901] 518, n. 5).

[82] Cf. W. Richter, *Traditionsgeschichtliche Untersuchungen zum Richterbuch* (BBB 18; Bonn, 1963) 92, 98.

a war of local importance between peoples north of the central hills. It was not a conflict between the whole population of the highlands and the Canaanites.[83] The poet, however, has tried to make it a conflict which involved all the forefathers of the Israelites of his time. For him, it became an all-Israelite event, so he used the names of the peoples who belonged to Israel during his own day.[84]

From the preceding discussion, it is easy to conclude that an analysis of the organization of the pre-monarchic Israel is an impossible task, since it consisted of several different groups of people who lived in the territory called Israel (i.e., the central highlands).[85] Only at the point when Israel emerges as a political unit, a nation, can one begin to discuss an Israelite political organization. In the earlier period, there

[83] Here we should mention that W. F. Albright has proposed that the word *pĕrāzôn*, 'peasant, villager,' in Judg 5:7 means 'warrior,' based on an assumed parallel to the Egyptian *prt* in the Papyrus Anastasi I 23:4 (*Yahweh and the Gods of Canaan* [Garden City, NY, 1968; reprint, Winona Lake, 1978] 49, n. 101). Cf. P. C. Craigie, "Some Further Notes on the Song of Deborah," *VT* 22 (1972) 350; and R. G. Boling, *Judges* (Anchor Bible 6A; Garden City, NY, 1975) 109. According to H. Cazelles, *prt* means 'to draw a bow' (with the left hand), "une manière anormale." Cazelles also sees a possible connection with the Perizzites of Gen 13:7 and 15:20, who lived in the territory of the Benjaminites, the left hand slingers ("Trois asiatismes possible dans Anastasi I," *Comptes rendues du group linguistique d'études Chamito-Sémitiques* Tome 9 [1960] 1ff.). (I am indebted to Professor E. F. Wente for this information.) While the root of *prt* designates the act of drawing a bow it does not necessarily follow that only warriors used bows. Villagers would have used them to hunt and to defend themselves. For the meaning 'peasant, villager' in Judg 5:7, cf. Ezek 38:11, Zech 2:3[8] and 1 Sam 6:18. See also G. F. Moore, *Judges* (ICC; Edinburgh, 1875) 144.

[84] Cf. my "Judges 5:20f. and History," 288. S. Herrmann maintains that the "document should not be over-estimated or seen in the context of a 'system' of tribes" (*A History of Israel*, 118). As to Judg 4:4–22, D. F. Murray claims that even though there may be a "hero-saga" behind the story in this text, this is only "the basic stuff out of which our narrator has woven an intricate pattern of plot and theme, a structure in which the inherent irony of the situation between the two men and the two women has become the dominant motif" ("Narrative Structure and Technique in the Deborah-Barak Story [Judges IV 4–22]" [VTSup 30; Leiden, 1979] 186).

[85] One of the few topics which can be discussed is the role of the elders of the different communities. See below, chap. 7.

may have been clan organizations, cities led by elders, city-states (Shechem and Jerusalem), a city federation (Gibeon-ites), and small kingdoms, such as those ruled by Gideon, Micah, and Samuel. What has to be acknowledged is that the biblical writers have tried to impose a certain historiographic pattern on the pre-monarchic period, and in accordance with this scheme all the peoples who lived in the hills in the territory of Israel in the pre-monarchic period have been labeled Israelites.[86] It should be remembered, though, that Israel, when used as a label, does not denote ethnicity. The complexity of the ancestry of the Israelites and Judahites has been recognized even by the biblical writers. About four centuries after Jerusalem had been made the capital by David, the prophet Ezechiel can still say about the city: "Your father was an Amorite, and your mother a Hittite" (Ezek 16:3, cf. v 45). In addition, Hitties, Jebusites, Amorites, and Hivites are listed in Gen 10:15f. as having been ethnic components of the land of Canaan (cf. also Josh 12:8; 24:11).[87]

In light of the foregoing discussion, the increase in settlements in the central hill country of Palestine was a process which spanned a few hundred years and which had its roots in the social and political instability in the eastern Mediterranean, characterized by the wars between the Hittite empire and Egypt, as well as the migrations of the Sea Peoples, and feuds between different Syro-Palestinian city-states. The hills became a place of refuge for many, mainly Canaanites, Arameans, and Edomites in the south. One can conclude from the Merneptah "Israel Inscription" that the central hill country had been known as Israel already before Merneptah's time, and that peoples who moved up to the hills and settled there could therefore be called Israelites.[88]

[86] For this pan-Israelite concept, cf. K. Galling, Die Erwählungstraditionen Israels (BZAW 38; Giessen, 1928) 68ff.

[87] D. N. Freedman's theory that the area around Ebla and Haran was "the fatherland of the Israelites" is thus too one-sided and unrealistic ("Ebla and the Old Testament," SPDS, 327). What could be said is that the peoples of the central highlands must have had many fatherlands.

[88] A historian therefore cannot agree with the assertion of F. M. Cross that Israel's history begins "when Yahwism emerged from its mythopoetic environment" (Canaanite Myth and Hebrew Epic, 135).

With the peoples follows the culture. We have seen that the population picture was mixed and so we should not expect the culture to be exactly the same everywhere. Canaan was a country in which influences from both north and south have always been found. Thus, we expect a certain mixture also in the territory of Israel. Most of the gods of Syria-Palestine seem to have been worshiped there, and the main god of the territory is El, the head of the Canaanite pantheon, as is also clear from the name Israel. What has usually been termed Canaanite culture is the culture of the highlands too. Archaeological material supports the opinion that there was no break in religious traditions, as there was no real break in pottery and house building traditions. Thus, for both material and religious culture there is a continuum from the Late Bronze period into the Iron I age.[89] In this connection we should also note that the language of the land is labeled in the Bible, Canaanite, "the tongue of Canaan" (Isa 19:18).[90]

[89] W. G. Dever has proposed a *new* approach to Israelite religion, suggesting that it developed out of the LB II and Iron I cultures of Canaan, and that the so-called "normative" Yahwism of the biblical writers is a late monarchic phenomenon ("Material Remains and Cult in Ancient Israel: An Essay in Archaeological Systematics," in *The Word of the Lord Shall Go Forth* [ed. C. L. Meyers and M. O'Connor; Winona Lake, IN, 1983] 578f.). This is right, but neither of these two things are new. Normative Yahwism has been considered late by several scholars for a long time, including the Assyriologist H. W. F. Saggs (*The Encounter with the Divine in Mesopotamia and Israel* [London, 1978] 6, 21ff.). Concerning Dever's "new approach," I have always underscored the cultural continuum.

[90] The inquiries into Israelite culture and religion have been made mainly along purist lines and are suspicious of everything that assumedly could be non-Israelite. (See, for instance, G. E. Mendenhall, "Ancient Oriental and Biblical Law," *BA* 17 [1954] 26–46.) Such an approach denies Israel and Judah their place in the ancient Near Eastern cultural milieu, and also ignores the fact that Israel and Judah emerged in history within that milieu. For a critique of this kind of approach, see J. D. Levenson, "The Temple and the World," *Journal of Religion* 64 (1984) 279ff. Levenson states, for instance, that the "quest for the distinctive in Israel is a wild-goose chase. . . . Put anything Israelite into a time machine in reverse and you end up with something non-Israelite" (p. 281). Cf. also H. W. F. Saggs, *The Encounter with the Divine*, 4.

7

Israel: A National Name

With Saul's creation of a territorial state in the highlands, a new political era began and Palestine soon became the place for a nation, the likes of which had never been known there before. With the disappearance of Egyptian dominance, the highland peoples were given the possibility of developing their own community organizations and systems of subsistence. Unfortunately for them, the Philistines managed to fill the void left by the Egyptians in the west, and in the east they were faced with the danger of Ammonite expansion. In this situation, the settled population of the hills came together under the leadership of a gifted ruler, Saul.

Firm facts about the founding of Saul's kingdom are hard to find in the present biblical narrative which is mainly concerned with emphasizing that the kingship, from its inauguration, was to be subservient to the prophetic office,[1] the only true form of intermediation between the people of Israel and their god, Yahweh. This aim has been accomplished in part by using the historian's pattern of opposites to structure the conflict between Samuel and Saul.[2] Underlying this conflict may have been an actual conflict between

[1] For kingship as a divine institution willed by the deity, see, for instance, Pss 2:7; 89:4–5, 20ff.; and 132. These passages probably reflect more of the official royal ideology of Israel and Judah than do the writings of the Samuel-Saul narratives. Cf. my article, "Solomon, the Chosen One," *History of Religions* 8 (1968) 93ff.

[2] The same pattern is used to structure the conflict between Saul and David later on.

the petty ruler Samuel and the successful *gibbôr ḥayil*, Saul, who had become the leader of most of the population of the hills north of Jerusalem.[3] In spite of the overarching literary patterns and theological concerns in the Saulide materials, it is possible to see from the stories about Saul that he became a powerful force in the central highlands and that he built up a standing army, fighting off the Philistines in the west and the Ammonites in the east. We assume that the elders of several communities in various regions acknowledged Saul or made some agreement with him.

Saul may have been able to extend his power through treaty relationships with other groups of people. This seems to have been the case with the citizens of Jabesh-Gilead, and possibly the deliberations with the elders of Gilgal in 1 Sam 11:14 should be seen in the same light.[4] The existence of a treaty between Saul and Jabesh-Gilead is indicated by 2 Sam 2:5f., in which David is said to have reminded the people of Jabesh-Gilead about their treaty with King Saul, assuring them that as Saul's new successor he now would do the same good for them as Saul had done.[5] The area of Jabesh-Gilead was therefore in all probability a vassal territory to Saul.[6] The use of cremation by this population group (1 Sam

---

[3] The area south of Jerusalem, including perhaps Bethlehem, was under the control of the Jebusite ruler, whose power was terminated finally by David. Cf. my article, "Was David a Jebusite Subject?" *ZAW* 92 (1980) 285ff. and J. L. McKenzie, "The Sack of Israel," 30. This means that Saul's power had not extended south of the Jebusite territory.

[4] For the council of elders as an authoritative political institution which also had cultic duties, see H. Klengel, "Die Rolle der 'Ältesten' (LÚ^{meš}ŠU.GI) im Kleinasien der hethiterzeit," *ZA* 57 (1965) 223–36; de Vaux, *Ancient Israel, its Life and Institutions* (New York, 1961) 137f., 152f.; G. W. Ahlström, *Joel and the Temple Cult of Jerusalem* (VTSup 21; Leiden, 1971) 35f.; M. Heltzer, *The Rural Community in Ancient Ugarit* (Wiesbaden, 1976) 79; G. Bettenzoli, "Gli 'Anziani' in Guida," *Biblica* 64 (1983) 211–24; F. Frick, *The City in Ancient Israel* (SBL Diss. Ser. 36; Missoula, MT, 1977) 114f.

[5] See D. Hillers, "A Note on Some Treaty Terminology in the Old Testament," *BASOR* 176 (1964) 46f.; Diana Edelman, "Saul's Rescue of Jabesh-Gilead (1 Sam. 11:1–11): Sorting Story from History," *ZAW* 96 (1984) 201ff.

[6] Its status as a vassal also tends to indicate that Saul was already king when he received the messengers from Gilead, 1 Samuel 11.

31:11ff.)[7] tends to confirm that they did not share the customs of the peoples of the central Israelite highlands and suggests that they were not originally part of an Israelite society, in spite of their characterization as tribal members in 1 Samuel 11.

Saul may have established treaty relationships with other peoples of neighboring territories, thereby extending his power base. The stronger he became, the more areas would have submitted to him.[8] The confirmation of the kingship by the ⁽am, 'the people,' in 1 Sam 11:14f. may be part of such a treaty relationship, as mentioned above. David's later rebuilding and expansion of Saul's kingdom was done in the same way. The growth of the kingdoms of Saul and David resembles the story about Idrimi of Alalakh's rise to kingship. He is said to have become king over "the country of Niᵓ, the country of Amaᵓu, the country of Mukish, and the city of Alalakh."[9] This inscription does not, however, reflect the actual deeds of Idrimi. It may be a fiction by the scribe, Šarruwa since he uses a certain literary style for expressing the rise of a successful king of the past. According to J. M. Sasson, this scribe "was at the vanguard of a literary style, probably originating somewhere in Northern Syria."[10] This

---

[7] The text states that they also buried their bones. It is not clear if this is a later addition or whether it refers to the ashes. It may demonstrate the author's abhorrence of cremation, which was not an Israelite practice, as far as can be determined. To an Israelite, cremation would have lead to extinction, preventing the dead person from having an afterlife.

[8] One group which is mentioned specifically in 1 Sam 14:21 to have gone over to Saul is the Hebrews, who seem to have been the population of the hills, Canaanites, or "Israelites." Unfortunately, the text does not detail the form of relationship by which they became associated with Saul.

[9] S. Smith, *The Statue of Idri-mi* (London, 1949) 16f., lines 37f.; cf. G. Buccellati, *Cities and Nations of Ancient Syria* (Studi Semitici 26; Rome, 1967) 139. See also M. S. Drower, "Syria c. 1550–1400 B.C.," *CAH³* II/1 (Cambridge, 1973) 433–35. For the literary pattern of the tale of Idri-mi, see Liverani, "Memorandum on the Approach to Historiographic Texts," 182f.

[10] J. M. Sasson, "On Idrimi and Šarruwa, the Scribe," in *Studies on the Civilization and Culture of Nuzi and the Hurrians in Honor of Ernest R. Lacheman* [ed. by M. A. Morrison and D. I. Owen; Winona Lake, IN, 1981] 323). Sasson states that the statue with the inscription is from the last phase

kind of literary style may also have been known and utilized in Palestine. We cannot, therefore, determine exactly how much truth there is in the stories about the growth of the kingdoms of Saul and David. Some exaggeration should be expected.

There is, however, one matter about the territories of Saul which should be taken into consideration here. In 2 Sam 2:9 we learn about the territories which were under Saul's rule and their possible relationship to the crown. Saul's son and successor, Eshbaal, is said to have reigned over Gilead, the Ashurites, Jezreel, and over Ephraim, Benjamin, and Israel. Since the preposition ʾel, 'to, for,' is used with the first three names, but ʿal is used with the last three, presumably some form of distinction in status is being made.[11] If we note that Saul is anointed king ʿal yiśrāʾēl, 'over Israel,' in 1 Sam 15:17,[12] the preposition ʾel (in 2 Sam 2:9) could perhaps be seen to mark territories which had come under the crown after Saul had been anointed king.

The last three areas named in the list—Ephraim, Benjamin, and Israel—probably represented the heartland of the kingdom. Gilead, the land of the Ashurites, and Jezreel by contrast, may have been areas which were added by treaty or by occupation. Since most of the territory was in the central highlands (i.e., Israel), it is understandable that Israel now became a name for a political entity, a nation.[13]

The location of the land of the Ashurites, mentioned in 2 Sam 2:9, is not clear. The reference has been associated, for instance, with the territory of Asher in the western

---

(Alalakh IB) of the city and the Ishtar temple, i.e., the inscription was made shortly before ca. 1200 B.C. (pp. 322ff.). Cf. also Van Seters, *In Search of History*, 188ff. For the text, see E. L. Greenstein and D. Marcus, "The Akkadian Inscription of Idrimi," *Journal of the Ancient Near Eastern Society of Columbia University* 8 (1976) 59–96, and, for a comparison with Jephthah and David, pp. 75–77.

[11] For a discussion of these problems, see Diana Edelman, "The 'Ashurites' of Eshbaal's State (2 Sam 2:9)," *PEQ* 117 (1985) 88ff.

[12] Cf. 1 Kgs 12:17.

[13] Cf. S. Herrmann, who states that "the area outlined in II Sam. 2.9 was given and continued to bear the name 'Israel.'" Judah was "never 'Israel' in the strict sense" (*A History of Israel*, 148).

Galilee, north of Carmel.[14] Looking at the structure of v 9, Gilead and Ephraim seem to be linked together as the main areas on each side of the Jordan River. The Ashurites and Benjamin could then be grouped together as the two smaller areas in Cisjordan. Alliteration tends to link Jezreel and *yiśrā'ēl*, the two remaining names, which otherwise contrast in their size. Jezreel is the (smallest?) addition to the territory of (Saul)-Eshbaal, while Israel is the largest and may also represent the totality (*kullōh*).

The Ashurites are mentioned in two other places in the Old Testament. In Gen 25:3, they are listed as the sons of Dedan, i.e., descendants of Abraham and Keturah. Thus, they are seen as Arabs.[15] The name also occurs in Ps 83:9[10] in a passage (vv 7–9[8–10]) mentioning a coalition of neighboring nations and peoples against Yahweh and his people, Israel. Although the text is probably post-exilic,[16] it indicates that a people named Ashur still existed in Transjordan. The use of Ashur in this verse has usually been seen as a reference to the Neo-Assyrian empire.[17] This is hardly probable. At no point in time did Assyria enter into an

[14] Cf. M. Noth, "Das Land Gilead als Siedlungsgebiet israelitischer Sippen," *Palästinajahrbuch* 37 (1941) 92f.; Aharoni, *The Land of the Bible*, 255.

[15] Cf. I. Eph'al, *The Ancient Arabs* (Leiden, 1982) 61. H. Gunkel felt that the Ashurites, Letusites, and Leumites of Gen 25:3 were later additions because of their absence from 1 Chr 1:32f. (*Die Urgeschichte und die Patriarchen* [*das erste Buch Mosis*) [2nd ed.; Göttingen, 1921] 179; and *Die Psalmen* [Göttingen, 1926] 365; cf. C. Westermann, *Genesis* [BK I:17] [Neukirchen-Vluyn, 1980] 485). E. Edel thinks that the Ashurites of Gen 25:3 are the Dedanites who are known from the caravan trade in North Arabia and locates them in the Hejaz district, but thinks that they may have been farther north in earlier times as well, for example, during the reign of Amenhotep III (*Die Ortsnamenlisten aus dem Totentempel Amenhophis III* [BBB 25; Bonn, 1966] 31; cf. S. Herrmann, *A History of Israel*, 52, n. 13). Diana Edelman suggests that these Ashurites were the Asherite enclave in the western Ephraimite foothills ("The 'Ashurites of Eshbaal's State (2 Sam 2:9)," 85–91. J. Grønbaek considers *h'šry* to be an anachronism and reads "Asser" (*Die Geschichte vom Aufstieg Davids (1. Sam 15–2. Sam 5)* [Copenhagen, 1971] 226).

[16] For a post-exilic date, cf. E. A. Leslie, *The Psalms* (New York and Nashville, 1949) 247f.

[17] Cf. H.-J. Kraus, *Psalmen* (BK XV:2) (Neukirchen-Vluyn, 1960) 82f.; M. Dahood, *Psalms 51–100* (Anchor Bible 17; Garden City, NY, 1968) 272.

alliance with Edom, Moab, Ammon, Amalek, Philistia, and the Phoenicians to fight Israel or Judah. Instead, it subdued them all, making them either vassals or incorporated provinces. In addition, it is hard to see Assyria as a servant of Lot, as v 8 characterizes the Ashurite group.[18] The reference to the "tents" of Edom, the Ishmaelites, Moab, and the Hagarites may indicate that the text dated from a time when the nations of Edom and Moab had ceased to exist and Arab tribes had made their inroads there. This would fit the time after the Babylonian destruction of Judah. Nehemiah mentions that the neighboring peoples were moving into the hills from the east, southeast, and west which resulted in mixed marriages (Neh 13:23ff.). Archaeological remains indicate that the Phoenicians had penetrated the foothills and the Sharon plain in the Persian period.[19]

If Ps 83:6–9[7–10][20] is merely a liturgical listing of general enemies of Israel over the years, then Ashur could represent the Assyrian empire. If, however, the list represents the situation of a particular time period, the post-exilic period is the only logical candidate. In this case, the name Ashur is best understood as a reference to an Arab tribe in Transjordan. With this in mind, it is possible that the deuteronomist had in mind the Transjordanian Ashurites of his own time when he wrote about the territories of Eshbaal in 2 Sam 2:9. This means, then, that of the three groups which are listed as vassals of Saul (Gilead, the Ashurites, and Jezreel), the first two were located in Transjordan (fig. 3).

[18] It should be mentioned that the LXX reads "Geshurites" instead of Ashurites in 2 Sam 2:9. This reading, however, contradicts the information in 2 Sam 3:3 and 13:37 which indicates that Geshur was an independent kingdom.

[19] Cf. Stern, *Material Culture of the Land of the Bible in the Persian Period 538–332 B.C.*, 239ff.

[20] Ps 83:7–8 has the following sequence:

the tents of Edom and the Ishmaelites, Moab and the Hagarites,
Gebal (or: the territory of) Ammon and Amalek,
Philistia with the inhabitants of Tyre,
also Ashur has joined up with them; they (= all) are the strength of Lot's children.

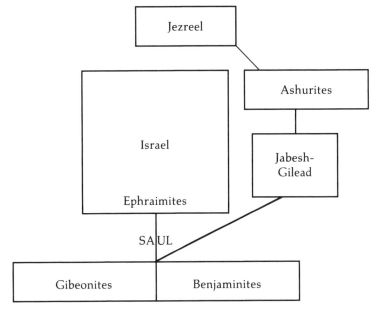

Fig. 3

The information in 2 Sam 2:9 may be trustworthy because it does not glorify Saul's rise to kingship. Instead, it laconically mentions the territories that his son Eshbaal "inherited." Instead, Saul's kingdom probably decreased in size after his death and some parts again came under the rule of the Philistines (cf. 1 Sam 31:7).

The scope of the Cisjordanian vassal, Jezreel, is impossible to ascertain from the context. Saul certainly did not rule over the old Canaanite cities of this area and presumably the eastern part of the Jezreel valley with Mount Gilboa had come under Saul's control. Jezreel's inclusion in the list offers an explanation as to the location of Saul's last battle against the Philistines at Mount Gilboa. He obviously wanted to expand his rule over the northern territories. The Philistines, however, who saw their power and trade being threatened in the area, managed to stop the expansion of Saul's kingdom. This means that Saul did not rule over the peoples of Galilee, a conclusion supported by 1 Chr 12:40[41] which mentions that Israel's neighbors were Naphtali, Zebulon, and Issachar.

To this territorial information, we should add the further indications of 1 Sam 14:47f. In addition to his battles against the Ammonites, the Philistines, and the Amalekites, Saul is reported to have campaigned successfully against the Moabites, the Edomites, and the Arameans ("the kings of Zobah") also. This verse has the character of an annalistic statement. If its information is historically reliable, Saul must be seen as the first empire builder in ancient Palestine. This fact has not been preserved, of course, by the pro-Davidic writers of the narratives, and since Saul's kingdom fell apart at his death and only the areas listed in 2 Sam 2:9 remained loyal to his son Eshbaal, the glory of building the great kingdom of Israel could be ascribed to David with some justification, ignoring Saul's previous accomplishments.

Yahweh became the main god of this new kingdom, Israel. The history of the early Yahwistic cult is impossible to outline. As has been mentioned above, Yahweh may have entered Palestine with a group from the Edomite territory (Seir, Paran, Teman) (cf. Deut 33:2; Judg 5:4; Hab 3:3).[21] We also note that the biblical traditions do not advocate unanimously that Yahweh had led his people out of Egypt. The so-called "Song of Moses" does not know the story about the Exodus from Egypt; instead, it claims that Yahweh found his people in the wilderness (Deut 32:10).

Yahweh's connection with Edom is also found in the story of the Ark's journey from the Philistines to Kiriath-jearim and, eventually, to Jerusalem. As was mentioned above, Yahweh seems to have been at home at Kiriath-jearim (1 Sam 7:1f.). After David's first attempt to move it to Jerusalem, the ark had been placed temporarily in the house (temple) of Obed-Edom (2 Sam 6:6–13). The name Obed-Edom could indicate that its bearer was a priest of the goddess Edom.[22] This suggestion is strengthened by the

[21] Cf. above, pp. 7f.

[22] For this goddess, see, among others, W. W. Baudissin, *Adonis and Esmun* (Leipzig, 1911) 45; S. A. Cook, *The Religion of Ancient Palestine in the*

mention of another Obed-Edom in 2 Chr 25:24, who was in charge of (ᶜ*im-*ᶜ*obed* ᵓ*ĕdôm*) a temple in Jerusalem which appears to be separate from the main Solomonic one.[23] This tends to indicate that the goddess Edom had been worshiped in Jerusalem at one time. Because Yahweh's ark was placed in her temple, she may have served as his consort, which would be consistent with his Edomite origin.

Since Kiriath-jearim appears to have been the home of the Ark of Yahweh, it seems that Yahweh had intimate connections with the Gibeonites, even though the origins of this association cannot be traced in the biblical texts. Yahweh could therefore have been the main deity of the famous *bāmāh* of Gibeon, which became the most important official sanctuary in the kingdom of Israel before the building of the Solomonic temple, according to 1 Kings 3. His rise to the position of the most important god of the new kingdom of Israel is perhaps best explained by assuming that Gibeon was Saul's hometown, as 1 Chr 9:35–38 imply.

David moved the Ark of Yahweh from Kiriath-jearim into Jerusalem to demonstrate that his state was a continuation of Saul's. Just as Yahweh had been the main god of Saul's nation, so now he was to continue as the national god under the new Davidic regime. This was part of David's legitimation plan. Under David, Yahweh became an imperial god. Like Marduk, who emerged at a certain point in time as king over all the Babylonian gods and also received their

---

Light of Archaeology (The Schweich Lectures on Biblical Archaeology, 1925; London, 1930) 112, cf. also 109; E. G. Kraeling, "The Real Religion of Israel," *JBL* 47 (1938) 156, n. 81; Albright, *Yahweh and the Gods of Canaan*, 140. For ᵓ*a-tu-m* referring to the consort of Resheph in Egyptian texts, see Helck, *Die Beziehungen*, 469. The chthonic character of this deity may be expressed by her name or epithet; ᵓ*dm* means 'red, dark soil,' cf. Hebrew ᵓ*ădāmāh* and Akkadian *adamātu*. Was she the mother goddess, "Mother Earth"? In light of the phrase from Kuntillet ᶜAjrud, "Yahweh and his Asherah," it is possible that Edom was identified with Asherah in Canaan. In this connection, it should be noted that Resheph was sometimes associated with *Qudšu* in Egypt (see W. J. Fulco, *The Canaanite God Rešep* [American Oriental Society Essays, 8; New Haven, 1976] 23f.).

[23] Cf. my article, "The Travels of the Ark," 146.

names,[24] Yahweh emerged as the highest of the deities of Canaan and became El Elyon or Yahweh Elyon (Pss 7:17[18]; 97:9; cf. Pss 9:2[3]; 57:2[3]; 92:1[2]). Zedek and Shalem were other names which could now be used for Yahweh. It was only after David had established his rule over the whole country and moved Yahweh to Jerusalem that he would have become the highest god of the land, the head of the divine assembly of Canaan. From that point in time, the plural form *ʾĕlôhîm* could be used as a name for Yahweh because he then embodied everything divine, just as the Akkadian plural *ilāni* could sometimes be used to refer to one god.[25] Thus, the phrase *ʾĕlohē yiśrāʾēl*, 'god of Israel,' did not come into use before the Davidic period.[26]

When the non-Israelite[27] David became king in Hebron, having forced himself on the peoples of the southern hills, he systematically worked at expanding his kingdom. One of his first acts was to attempt to get the men of Jabesh-Gilead to acknowledge him as their new king by transferring their previous treaty relationship with Saul to him (2 Sam 2:5ff.). Another early act was his slaughter of several of Saul's descendants at Gibeon to appease the Gibeonites and thus to avert any possible rebellion on their part. After both Abner

[24] Consult W. G. Lambert, "The Reign of Nebuchadnezzar I: A Turning Point in the History of Ancient Mesopotamian Religion," in *The Seeds of Wisdom, Essays in Honor of T. J. Meek* (ed. W. S. McCullough; Toronto, 1964) 3ff.; W. W. Hallo and J. J. A. van Dijk, *The Exaltation of Inanna* (New Haven, 1968) 66f.

[25] Anne E. Drafkorn (Kilmer), "Ilani/Elohim," *JBL* 76 (1957) 216ff., and cf. my article, "The Travels of the Ark," 147ff.

[26] This would mean that the Song of Deborah would be much later than is commonly assumed, because this phrase occurs in v 3 as an epithet of Yahweh.

[27] See Ahlström, "Was David a Jebusite Subject?" 285ff. The Book of Ruth preserves a tradition which considered David to have been of Moabite descendancy (Ruth 4:18–22). It is probable that the author of Ruth has tried to depict Ruth as a devoted Yahweh worshiper so that later generations would accept it as a fact. The book therefore should be seen as a defense for David, whose Moabite blood would have been unacceptable to the post-exilic society, in which Moabites were explicitly excluded from membership in Yahweh's congregation (Deut 23:3–6).

and Eshbaal, Saul's son, had been murdered—perhaps with his blessing—he was successful in having the men of Israel make a treaty with him in Hebron and elect him king.[28] He took the Jebusite city of Jerusalem and made it the capital of his new United Monarchy, thereby ending the independence of the Jebusites. With the control of this city, he inherited an old and well-established administrative apparatus, which naturally was advantageous to him.[29]

According to 1 Chr 12:38–40[39–41], the territories of Issachar, Zebulon, and Naphtali were not considered part of Israel. This passage states that the men of Israel came to Hebron accepting David as their king. It adds that "also their neighbors as far as Issachar and Zebulon and Naphtali came with food. . . ." This statement of the Chronicler clearly shows that to an Israelite these peoples of the Jezreel Valley and the territories north of it were not considered Israelites because they did not live in the territory of Israel, i.e., the central highlands. These northern peoples first became nominally Israelites during the time of David.

Remaining Canaanite territories such as Asher in the Galilee and some parts of the Philistine area,[30] as well as the Transjordanian territory of Gad may have become part of the new kingdom. In this period of territorial expansion, David must have taken such cities as Megiddo and Tell Abu Hawam,[31] Dor, Beth-Shan, Beth-Shemesh, and Tell Qasîle and perhaps some areas north of the Galilee, such as the Beqaᶜ valley. They all may have been added to the kingdom either by military or diplomatic means. In other words, David's kingdom became so great that previously unconquered areas and cities of Canaan were surrounded, necessitating their surrender to the new power in Jerusalem. We

[28] Cf. the discussion by J. C. Vanderkam, "Davidic Complicity in the Deaths of Abner and Eshbaal," *JBL* 99 (1980) 521–39.

[29] Cf. Ahlström, *Royal Administration*, 27ff.

[30] Cf. Ahlström, "The Travels of the Ark," 143f.

[31] For Abu Hawam's probable role as the port city of Megiddo, see Diane L. Saltz, "Greek Geometric Pottery in the East: The Chronological Implications" (Unpubl. diss., Harvard University); Cambridge, MA, 1978) 165ff.

also learn from the narratives that neighboring countries such as Edom, Moab, Ammon and some Aramean territories were subdued (cf. 2 Sam 8:12f.).

What was begun under Saul was thus repeated successfully and increased under David. Smaller units had to accept the more powerful one. They either were conquered or they submitted freely out of necessity. That is how an empire forms. We therefore can call Saul the first empire builder in Palestine. Unfortunately for him, his kingdom fell apart, but David, his officer and son-in-law who had tried to usurp the throne,[32] successfully followed in his footsteps and enlarged the kingdom even further. It is under David that the first real conquest of Canaan occurred after the end of the Egyptian rule in the region. With David's kingdom all of the inhabitants of Canaan (except the Philistines) became nominal Israelites.

As a result of David's conquests and political treaties and Solomon's diplomacy and trade connections, the cultural and economic isolation of the peoples of the hills was broken. Solomon's building programs in Jerusalem and other cities in his empire were influenced architecturally and artistically by Syro-Phoenician culture. This is understandable, since the hill country had not seen much of this before. We should note that the hills were probably still the most sparsely populated parts of the country and that their population consisted mainly of agriculturalists. Their cultural achievements, therefore, would not have been as advanced as those in the lowlands and coastal areas. Monumental buildings, fortresses, fortified cities, store cities, and decorative art in general had not been an integral part of the material culture of these mountain peoples. The architectural layout for these types of structures and the technical skill to build them would have had to have been borrowed from neighboring cultures, such as the Phoenicians who, in turn, had been influenced greatly by Egyptian culture.[33]

[32] See M. Cohen, "The Role of the Shilonite Priesthood in the United Monarchy of Israel," *HUCA* 36 (1965) 59–98.

[33] North of the Jezreel Valley, more Syrian influence would have prevailed. See above, p. 36, n. 42. For building activities under David and

The new international culture which became a part of the life of the peoples of the mountains during the United Monarchy would have been limited to urban centers; villagers, who were conservative by nature, were probably untouched by most of these new things. Having originally left the urban and industrial districts of Canaan, they would have developed new customs in response to the demands of their new environment. While their material culture would have basically remained Canaanite, it would have developed its own adaptations which would have remained consistent because of their conservatism and continuing hostility to the old urban cultural practices and peoples. Presumably, the material culture of both Israel and Judah in the period after their split, when they constituted small kingdoms enclosed in the hills, became somewhat impoverished. This would have been true especially in the villages, even though these nations were branches of the general culture of Canaan with its Phoenicio-Egyptian features. The economic, cultural, and religious hostility voiced by the Hebrew prophets can be seen as an expression of the isolation of these mountain peoples and their search for identity and independence.

When Solomon died, the union between Israel and Judah fell apart. From that point on, Israel became an independent political unit. The immediate cause of the break was Solomon's treatment of Israel as a vassal; she simply wanted her freedom. Israel and Judah had never fused together, however, and the treatment by the king, the royal court, and its officials had been such that rebellion seemed to be the only way out. One of Solomon's highest officials, Jeroboam, is said to have "lifted his hand" (i.e., rebelled) against the king. He did not succeed, and fled to Egypt, where he was well-received by pharaoh Shoshenq (1 Kgs 11:26–40). Shoshenq obviously was a man who had his eyes open for possible expansions of the power of Egypt, and Jeroboam became an opportune tool for his expansion.[34]

Solomon in particular, see W. G. Dever, "Monumental Architecture in Ancient Israel in the Period of the United Monarchy," *SPDS*, 269–306.

[34] Cf. the discussion in C. D. Evans, "Naram-Sin and Jeroboam: The Archetypal *Unheilscherrscher* in Mesopotamian and Biblical Historiography,"

Jeroboam returned to Palestine after Solomon's death, and presumably with the blessings of Pharaoh, he helped Israel throw off the yoke of the king in Jerusalem. Rehoboam's attempt to establish himself as his father's successor over both Judah and Israel had failed. He had gone to Shechem to renew the Israelite treaty and to reforge the union between Judah and Israel (1 Kgs 12:1ff.). After the Israelites had rejected his conditions, he made the mistake of sending the chief of forced labor, Adoram, the most hated man in Israel, to deal with them, probably by continuing the levy conscriptions. Adoram was stoned to death, and only then did the king understand the situation. He quickly mounted his chariot and covered the distance to Jerusalem, probably in record time. In this way the artificial bond between Israel and Judah was severed forever (1 Kgs 12:18f.).

Five years later (ca. 926 B.C.), pharaoh Shoshenq campaigned in Palestine, using border skirmishes with Semites as his excuse for a large-scale invasion. All we learn from the Bible about this campaign is that Rehoboam had to pay the pharaoh most of the treasure of the royal palaces and temple to maintain his throne (1 Kgs 14:25ff.). We can conclude from Shoshenq's list of conquered cities that he did not do much campaigning in Judah proper. Most of the places which are listed were in the Negev, Israel, and parts of Transjordan, which belonged to Israel. Following S. Herrmann, it is assumed that Shoshenq marched along the trunk road up to Megiddo and that either en route or after his arrival, he sent out detachments to different parts of the country, like Jerusalem and Tell Abu Hawam,[35] for instance.[36] Since Jerusalem is not named in the list, one can assume that Rehoboam capitulated before any siege was laid to the city.

---

in *Scripture in Context II: More Essays on the Comparative Method* (ed. W. W. Hallo, J. C. Moyer, L. G. Perdue; Winona Lake, IN, 1983) 114ff.

[35] Cf. K. A. Kitchen, *The Third Intermediate Period in Egypt (1100–650 B.C.)* (Warminster, 1973) 299, 437 n. 73. Cf., also, Saltz, "Greek Geometric Pottery in the East," 165f.

[36] S. Herrmann, "Operationen Pharao Schoschenks I. im östlichen Ephraim," *ZDPV* 80 (1964) 55–79.

The intriguing question here is why it took Shoshenq five years to decide to attempt to undermine the power of the kingdoms of Israel and Judah. Why did he not take action immediately after Solomon's death and see to it that the Solomonic empire was crushed once and for all? Why did he campaign more in Israel and the Negev than in Judah proper? His reason for taking the Negev is apparent: he wanted to terminate the Jerusalemite-Phoenician trade alliance to the Gulf of Aqabah, thus making Egypt master of trade on the Red Sea once again. His lack of interest in Judah proper, is puzzling, however, and the Bible's silence about Jeroboam's defense against the Egyptian invasion is equally curious. Did Jeroboam run away and let the pharaoh take whatever cities and areas he wanted? With most of the chariots and manpower of the former Solomonic empire in his possession, we would expect him to have defended his country. This raises some questions. Was Jeroboam unable to establish himself as king? Had the wars with Rehoboam weakened his position to the point that Shoshenq felt that Rehoboam might regain supremacy over the lost northern territories? This is one possible explanation of the data.[37] Another possible contributing factor may have been Jeroboam's repudiation of Egyptian vassalage, leading Shoshenq to teach him a lesson and show him who his master was.

Whatever the answers to these questions, the Egyptian invasion in 926 B.C. made the split of Solomon's kingdom permanent. Palestine was once again a territory of small nations. Israel lived on as an independent nation for more than a century and became more powerful than the kingdom of Judah, which almost became her vassal under the Omride regime. After the division, the political name Israel referred only to the northern kingdom and thus, the term Israelites could no longer include the people of the south, Judah.

[37] Cf. T. H. Robinson, *A History of Israel* I (Oxford, 1932) 275.

8

Israel: An Ideological Term

The investigation thus far has shown that the name Israel began as a territorial term, and then became a political term designating the state in the central hill country north of Jerusalem which was first established by Saul. After subsequent expansion under David and Solomon during the period when it was joined to Judah by treaty and shared the same king (the United Monarchy), it became the independent Northern Kingdom until 722 B.C. The name also took on a theological dimension in that it represented the people of Yahweh, the *qĕhal yiśrā'ēl*, the cultic congregation (cf. Josh 8:35, 1 Kgs 8:14, 22, 55; Mic 2:5; Joel 2:16). This arose from the common ancient conception that the god's political nation also constituted his cultic congregation because he ruled over and protected that group, both politically and religiously.[1] Although Israel as a political term was almost always restricted to the Northern Kingdom after the split of the United Monarchy,[2] it could be used as a theological

[1] Another phrase which should be noted is *kol yiśrā'ēl*, which we meet in several passages in the historical book. It expresses the tendency of the biblical writers to identify the religious ideal which made Israel the people of Yahweh, with the political situation, real or imaginary. For *qāhāl* as a socio-religious term, especially applied to the post-exilic cultic community, see S. Mowinckel, *Studien zu dem Buche Ezra-Nehemiah* I (SNVAO II. Hist.-Filos. Klasse. Ny Serie No. 3; Oslo, 1964) 86ff.; J. D. W. Kritzinger, *Q'hal Yahwe* (Kampen, 1957); H. W. Wolff, *Joel* (BK XIV:5; Neukirchen-Vluyn, 1963) 60.

[2] Statistically, Israel is used 564 times in the Old Testament for the Northern Kingdom, in contrast to 17 instances where it seems to refer to

designation for the populations of both Israel and Judah, since Yahweh continued to serve as the national god of both political units.[3]

After Israel's demise as a political and religious entity in 722 B.C. and the conversion of its core territory into the Assyrian province of Samerina, southern prophetic circles began to preempt the name Israel for the nation of Judah. Proto-Isaiah, one of the first to do so, used the phrase, *qĕdôš yiśrā'ēl*, 'the holy one of Israel,' as an epithet of Yahweh of Judah twelve times (cf. also 2 Kgs 19:22). It is possible that this phrase was heard in the liturgy of the sanctuaries and this may account for its occurrences in some Psalms such as 71:22, 78:41, 89:18[19], cf. 22:3[4]. The *trishaggion* in Isa 6:3 may be another indication. The holiness of Yahweh is stressed in so many texts that it is quite natural to assume that such an emphasis was part of the worship. The prophetic use of the phrase *qĕdôš yiśrā'ēl* is most probably inspired by this picture of Yahweh as the holy one. We should note that this phrase appears, furthermore, thirteen times in the later Isaian writings, twice in Jeremiah, and once in Ezekiel. Isaiah also spoke of the "two houses of Israel" (8:14), clearly using the name in a religious sense. Jeremiah characterized Judah as *bᵉtûlat yiśrā'ēl*, 'the young woman, Israel' in Jer 31:21. Similarly, Deutero-Isaiah claimed that Israel would become a name of honor for a Judahite (44:5). Zechariah used Israel to represent both Jerusalem and Judah (12:1) and maintained that the people of Judah constituted the remnant of Yahweh's people, Israel (cf. 8:6). In the prophetic writings, then, the theological dimension of the name Israel, in which Israel represents Yahweh's people, began to be developed and stressed.[4]

---

the Southern Kingdom. See H.-J. Zobel, "יִשְׂרָאֵל, *jiśrā'el*," *TWAT* (Stuttgart, 1982) col. 994.

[3] Cf. G. A. Danell, *Studies in the Name Israel in the Old Testament* (Uppsala, 1946) 155ff. Hosea uses Israel to designate the people of the Northern Kingdom religiously and Ephraim to designate them politically. Cf. H. W. Wolff, *Hosea* (BK XIV:1; Neukirchen-Vluyn, 1961) 212.

[4] For a résumé of the prophetic-religious use of the name, see Zobel, "יִשְׂרָאֵל, *jiśrā'el*," cols. 1006ff.

This trend continued and intensified after the destruction of the kingdom of Judah in 587/6 B.C. In particular, writers who had been exiled during the two Babylonian deportations were faced with developing a new form of Yahwism which was not bound to state and territory. In so doing, they came to focus on Israel as the cultic community of true Yahweh worshipers. With the return of some of this group to Judah and Jerusalem and their confrontation with the local population which had not been exiled and which did not share the theological precepts which had evolved in Babylonia, the term Israel took on a further restrictive sense. It came to designate primarily the cultic congregation of the returnees, in contrast to the peoples of the province of Judah, although it occasionally was used in a wider sense to include the Jews of the Diaspora, who shared the same theological understanding of Judaism which had emerged from the exilic experience.

After the devastation of Judah and, in particular, of Jerusalem and its environs, many, but not all, of the surviving Judahites were exiled. A portion of the native population, probably consisting mainly of poor peasants, was left behind in the land and the Babylonian king appointed Gedaliah, a member of the royal court of Jerusalem, as overseer (*pāqîd*) (2 Kgs 25:22). He made Mizpah the center of his administration. After only ca. three months in office, Gedaliah was murdered by a Davidic prince named Ishmael (2 Kgs 25:25)[5] and no information has been preserved about the form of government in the territory after this event. A new deportation took place in 582 B.C.[6] (Jer 25:30). It is possible that Judah then had such a small population that a new overseer or governor was not appointed, but instead, Judah became part of the province of Samerina until Sheshbazzar was appointed by the Persians.[7] One gets the impression that the

[5] According to Jer 40:14 (cf. 41:10, 15), the king of Ammon, Baalis, was behind this.

[6] Josephus mentions that Nebuchadrezzar put an end to the kingdoms of Ammon and Moab in the Syro-Palestinian expedition in his 23rd year (= 582 B.C.), incorporating them into his empire (*Antiq.* X, 9, 7).

[7] For the history of the Exile and the Persian period, see, among others, E. Meyer, *Die Entstehung des Judentums* (Halle, a.S. 1896); K. Galling,

territory was so impoverished and depopulated that it did not need its own administration. Judah was again a country without a state and without the feeling of nationhood that binds peoples together.

The demographic picture in Judah changed somewhat after the Babylonian devastation of the country. Edomites invaded the southern territory, having been pushed from their land by Arabs. This resulted in the southern half of Judah becoming Edomite and, eventually, the sub-province of Idumea, with Hebron its northernmost city.[8] We may also assume that Ammonites and Moabites took refuge in Cisjordan after the destruction of their nations in 582 B.C. Ammonite infiltration appears to have begun in the period immediately after 586 B.C., as indicated by King Baalis's interest in Judah in connection with the murder of Gedaliah. We also know from excavations that there was an increase in Phoenician presence in western Palestine during the early Persian period. Remains of houses with piers or monoliths "set at fairly regular intervals into rubble or ashlar"[9] have been uncovered around western Palestine, a

---

Studien zur Geschichte Israels im persischen Zeitalter (Tübingen, 1964); M. Avi-Yonah, *The Holy Land from the Persian to the Arab Conquest* (Grand Rapids, MI, 1966) 11–31; P. R. Ackroyd, *Exile and Restoration* (Philadelphia, 1968); G. Widengren, "The Persian Period," in *Israelite and Judean History* (ed. J. H. Hayes and J. M. Miller; Philadelphia, 1977) 489–538; P. R. Ackroyd, "The History of Israel in the Exilic and Post-Exilic Periods," in *Tradition and Interpretation* (ed. G. W. Anderson; Oxford, 1979) 320–50; and S. E. McEvenue, "The Political Structure in Judah from Cyrus to Nehemiah," *CBQ* 43 (1981) 353–64.

[8] For the unhistorical nature of Neh 11:25ff. (the expansion of the territory of Judah), see Meyer, *Die Entstehung des Judentums*, 132; Alt, "Judas Gaue unter Josia," 100ff. (= *KS* II, 280). It was only under the Hasmonean ruler John Hyrcanus (134–104 B.C.) that Idumea, including Hebron, became Jewish (by force).

[9] G. and O. Van Beek, "Canaanite-Phoenician Architecture: The Development and Distribution of Two Styles," *Eretz Israel* 15 (1981) 70*. This type of building also spread to Punic Tunisia and Algeria, see Van Beek and Van Beek, "Canaanite-Phoenician Architecture," 71*ff. For Palestine, also consult A. Ben-Tor, Y. Portugali, M. Avissar, "The Third and Fourth Seasons of Excavations at Tel Yokneᶜam, 1979 and 1981," *IEJ* 33 (1983) 33.

known Phoenician building technique. Phoenician-styled artifacts have been found at sites such as Tell ed-Duweir, Tell eṣ-Ṣafi, and Maresha,[10] allowing us to assume that Phoenicians spread inland (cf. Joel 4:4–6).[11] It is also likely that the Philistines took advantage of the situation and moved into some of the abandoned or destroyed areas and villages in the hilly areas (cf. Ezek 33:21ff.; 36:5; Joel 3[4]:4–6). Thus, when the small band of returnees arrived from Babylonia, they found a country that they did not know or recognize. They did not know its people or its mixture of different ethnic groups; presumably, language was the only trait that they had in common. Culturally and religiously, the two groups had become strangers.

The fairly complex demographic picture which can be reconstructed from archaeology and textual references contrasts sharply with the description of the situation in the Books of Ezra and Nehemiah. Two trends emerge in these writings. On the one hand, they ignore the ethnic complexity and lump all non-returnees into a single category, the ᶜam hāʾāreṣ, 'the people of the land,'[12] who are then contrasted with the gōlāh. The former group consisted of those who were later called Samaritans,[13] suggesting that the textual material was written down at a time when the

---

[10] Josephus mentions a Phoenician colony in the city of Shechem (*Antiq.* XI, 8, 6). For Galilee's sizable Phoenician population in the Persian period, see Stern, *Material Culture of the Land of the Bible in the Persian Period 538–332 B.C.*, 240.

[11] See H.-P. Müller, "Phönizien und Juda in exilisch-nach-exilischer Zeit," *Die Welt des Orients* 6 (1971) 189ff. For the time of Joel, see my *Joel and the Temple Cult of Jerusalem* (VTSup 21; Leiden, 1971) 111–29.

[12] For this phrase and its meanings, see A. Oppenheimer, *The ᶜam ha-aretz: A Study in the Social History of the Jewish People in the Hellenistic-Roman Period* (Arbeiten zur Literatur und Geschichte des hellenistischen Judentums 8; Leiden, 1977) 10ff. with citations. It often is mistakenly associated with "northerners." Ezra 6:21 seems to indicate that some of the local population were accepted into the gōlāh party; specifically, anyone who had "separated himself from the cultic pollution of the peoples of the land."

[13] H. G. M. Williamson considers Ezra 1–6 to be "counter-propaganda to the building of the first Samaritan temple on Mount Gerizim" ("The Composition of Ezra I–VI," *JTS* 34 [1984] 29).

conflict with the people of the north was actual.[14] The texts do not acknowledge any gap in time between the returns under Sheshbazzar and Zerubbaal and the rise of the *gōlāh* party in the days of Ezra-Nehemiah. Unless new source material becomes available, we will never learn what really happened in the period between 538 B.C. and the arrival of Nehemiah.[15]

On the other hand, the Book of Ezra indirectly acknowledges the existence of an ethnic mixture in the land in the post-exilic period in its discussion of the issue of mixed marriages, as does Neh 13:23–30. Ezra 9:1ff. claims that the officials complained to Ezra that the "people of Israel," the priests, and the Levites had taken wives from among the Canaanites, the Hittites, the Perizzites, the Jebusites, the Ammonites, the Moabites, the Egyptians, and the Amorites, who constituted the "peoples of the lands." We should note here the occurrence of many archaic terms for the "pre-Israelite" population groups of the country: Canaanites, Hittites, Perizzites, Jebusites, and Amorites (cf. Exod 23:20ff.).[16] Historically, there were no Jebusites in the post-exilic period, and any remnants of Perizzites, Hittites, and Amorites would have been overcome and absorbed by different Judahite clans at a much earlier time and lost their identity then.

[14] For the juxtaposition of materials from different decades in the late texts, making a reconstruction of the period's chronology almost impossible, see Ackroyd, *Exile and Restoration*, 138–217; Ackroyd, "Historical Problems of the Early Achaemenian Period," *Eastern Great Lakes Biblical Society/Proceedings* IV (Westerville, OH, 1984) 37–53; Widengren, "The Persian Period," 503–9; S. Japhet, "The Supposed Common Authorship of Chronicles and Ezra-Nehemiah Investigated Anew," *VT* 18 (1968) 330–71; and Japhet, "Sheshbazzar and Zerubbabel: Against the Background of the Historical and Religious Tendencies of Ezra-Nehemiah," *ZAW* 94 (1982) 66–98.

[15] The reference in Ezra 9:9 (Ezra's prayer) to a wall in Jerusalem and in Judah may indicate that Ezra arrived after Nehemiah. Even though the term *gādēr*, 'vineyard wall,' is used instead of the usual *ḥomāh*, 'city wall,' the impression is that the description of Judah as Yahweh's vineyard may have been influenced by the presence of the new city wall. Cf. Bright, *A History of Israel*, 395; Widengren, "The Persian Period," 504.

[16] Cf. J. Van Seters, "The Terms 'Amorite' and 'Hittite' in the Old Testament," *VT* 22 (1972) 64–81.

Since the returnees settled mainly in Jerusalem and its surroundings where there was virtually no existing population,[17] they could not have come into conflict with such groups as the Canaanites, Perizzites, and Hittites, even if they had continued to exist as distinctive enclaves, which is highly improbable.[18] These archaic terms appear elsewhere in the programmatic writings about the conquest, so that their use here in Ezra should probably be assigned to the same circle of post-exilic historiographers.[19] While the terms cannot be taken to reflect the historical situation, they nevertheless can be seen as indications that the returnees found themselves faced with a complex demographic picture when they returned to their old homeland.

The resettlement of Judahite territory during the exilic period by various groups who supplemented the non-exiled Judahites meant that the returnees were not free to re-occupy their old property. As the latest newcomers, they would have been considered *gērîm*, "foreigners," by the local population, and therefore would not have had any right to the land. This would have forced them to settle in areas which were still unoccupied—in the areas most severely devastated by the Babylonians and in areas which were not conducive to agriculture. We know from biblical texts that they resettled and rebuilt Jerusalem. Archaeological surveys

---

[17] For a concentration of small settlements south of Jerusalem in the Persian period, see, for instance, Kochavi et al., *Judea, Samaria, and the Golan,* and especially the map of Judea and its "Lists according to their Periods."

[18] In the period of Ezra and Nehemiah, the society encountered problems with Samaritans, Philistines, Edomites, and Transjordanians.

[19] See, for instance, S. Mowinckel, *Studien zu dem Buche Ezra-Nehemia* III, (SNVAO II:7; Oslo, 1965) 20. Two parallels between the exilic community's experiences and those which came to be part of the biblical narratives should be noted. First, both the group leaving Egypt for Canaan and the Ezra group returning to Judah have with them the law of their god. No wonder Ezra has been seen as another Moses! Secondly, Ezra's actions in the home country parallel those taken by Joshua during and after the occupation of the promised land in many respects. Cf. K. Koch, "Ezra and the Origins of Judaism," *JSS* 19 (1974) 188. These are indications that the Wilderness-Conquest theme and the Ezra writings originated in the same circles.

have discovered a concentration of small settlements south of Jerusalem proper dating from the Persian period which probably can be assigned to the group also.[20] The location of these villages was undoubtedly determined by both the availability of the land which was less desirable in nature and by the desire to form a close-knit enclave which would not be absorbed by the "strange" peoples of the land.

The unavailability of land which confronted the group of returnees probably gave rise to the tradition of the promise of the land to Abraham.[21] Because their right to the land was being questioned, they needed a basis by which they could claim it.[22] By extension, the conquest under Joshua is to be seen as the fulfillment of the promise of the land. In order to overcome the resistance of the people of the land, the writers of the *gōlāh* party appear to have appealed to a divine promise which was supposed to have been given in prehistoric times to Abraham, the ancestral father and symbol of the Jews. As Abraham had once left Mesopotamia and wandered to Canaan, so the people of the Exile had left and were re-entering the "land of promise." The archaic references to the early inhabitants in the area mentioned above

[20] Cf. Kochavi et al., *Judea, Samaria, and the Golan*, map and lists.

[21] For the land promise as an etiological text legitimizing the possession of the country, see W. M. Clark, "The Origin and Development of the Land Promise Theme in the Old Testament" (unpubl. Ph.D. diss., Yale University; New Haven, 1964) 98. Cf. C. Westermann, who sees the promise of the land and those in Genesis 12–50 to belong to the latest stage of composition ("Arten der Erzählung in der Genesis," *Forschung am Alten Testament. Gesammelte Studien* [Theologische Bücherei 24; Munich, 1964] 33); J. Van Seters, *Abraham in History and Tradition* (New Haven and London, 1975) 249–79. M. Anbar thinks Genesis 15 is a "conflation of two narratives . . . written by scribes of the deuteronomistic school, perhaps during the exile" ("Gen. 15: A Conflation of Two Deuteronomistic Narratives," *JBL* 101 [1982] 54f.).

[22] The promise in Gen 15:18 about an empire stretching from Egypt to Mesopotamia is nothing more than a dream about the resurrection of the Davidic empire. J. Van Seters has pointed to the fact that Ezek 20:5f. states that Yahweh promised the land of Canaan by oath to the people while they were in Egypt. Thus, the "modification of the promise theme to make it patriarchal is secondary and exilic" ("Confessional Reformation in the Exilic Period," *VT* 22 [1972] 454f.).

were included in the historiography of this group and period, possibly to emphasize that the groups currently in possession of the land were not the original owners but relative latecomers who also needed to justify their claim. The promise of the land and the conquest narratives are therefore to be seen as programmatic scripts of the *gōlāh* party.[23]

The Babylonian exile led to the reordering of religious thought about the presence of Yahweh among his people and the membership of his cultic community. Babylonia was not Yahweh's territory; both politically and religiously, Yahwistic worship had no place in Babylonia. The adoption of the worship of Babylonian gods would have been the natural response to the new situation, since it was normal practice to worship the gods of the land where one was living. The polemics in Deutero-Isaiah against Babylonian gods (40:19ff.) reflect an attempt to stem this growing tide in the exilic community, in fear that the abandonment of the worship of Yahweh would result in the extinction of Yahweh's people.[24] Faced with the possible loss of identity, the religious leaders of the exiles made the bold and radical

[23] In this connection, we should note that according to Joshua 22, there were "Israelites" who were forced to stay in Transjordan, who could not settle in the promised land. This has been understood as an idea originating with the deuteronomist in the post-exilic community; see R. Polzin, *Moses and the Deuteronomist* (New York, 1980); J. G. Vink, "The Date and Origin of the Priestly Code in the Old Testament," *Oudtestamentische Studien* 15 (1969) 73ff. A. D. H. Mayes views Josh 22:1–6 as a "deuteronomistic epilogue" (*The Story of Israel between Settlement and Exile* [London, 1983] 160, cf. 59). Joshua 22 indicates that the peoples of Transjordan did not belong to the post-exilic community of Judah. Nevertheless, some explanation had to be given in the history of the peoples of Yahweh as to why "Israelites" lived east of the Jordan, the river which divided the period of the "Wanderings in the Wilderness" from the settlement in Canaan, "the promised land." The altar which was built at the Jordan by non-Palestinian "Israelites" may be a veiled reference to the Elephantine cult. In this case, the chapter would be addressed to the Jews of the Diaspora. See the discussion by Vink, "The Date and Origin of the Priestly Code in the Old Testament," 73ff.

[24] Cf. Heike Friis, "Eksilet og den israelitiske historieopfattelse," *DTT* 38 (1975) 1f.

assertion that Yahweh was not bound to a state or a particular territory like other deities. Ezekiel, for instance, asserted that Yahweh had followed his people into exile and thus, could still be worshiped, even if the nation and its temple no longer existed (11:14ff.). Similarly, Deutero-Isaiah promised that Yahweh would return to Zion (52:8), and Nahum stated that Yahweh would return "together with the pride of Jacob" (2:2[3]).[25] One might say that the "congregational" idea of religion was born in the Exile to help the deported Judahites rationalize their circumstances. This concept would have been completely foreign to the Judahites who had not been exiled, however, and thus created conflict between the two groups after the *gōlāh* group returned.

With the return and resettlement of members of the exilic community in Jerusalem and its environs at various times under different leaders, the term Israel became yet narrower in scope. It designated the congregation of Yahweh's worshipers, and excluded the peoples of the land, even those Judahites who had never left the land since they did not share the *gōlāh* group's sectarian views which had developed in Babylonia. The biblical writers who belonged to this returning group, either as members or later descendants, expressed their views about the "true" Israel by branding the local population of the hills as "polluted" peoples, while singling out the *gōlāh* as the cream of the population, the "right" people of Yahweh, the true *qĕhal yiśrā'ēl*. Ezra, for example, uses Israel almost exclusively as

[25] Nahum's book concerns Assyria and the people in exile there. It is not clear whether Nahum uttered these words himself. His speech in 1:15–2:2[2:1–3] is suspiciously close to that of Isa 52:1–2, 7–8; cf. A. S. van der Woude, "The Book of Nahum: A Letter Written in Exile," *Oudtestamentische Studiën* 20 (Leiden, 1977) 116–19. The inclusion of the book of Nahum in the Twelve Prophets suggests that it was part of a post-exilic religious literary activity, which would have had the prophet who spoke to the Israelites in Assyria deliver the same ideas of restoration as were presented to those in exile in Babylonia. For Nahum as a literary product of the post-exilic period and its cult, cf. H. Schulz, *Das Buch Nahum: Eine redaktionskritische Untersuchung* (BZAW 129; Berlin, 1973) 133f.

an ideological term. Twenty-two of the twenty-four appearances of the name describe the people of Yahweh rather than a territory.[26] Judah and Jerusalem continue as territorial terms, with the (Aramaic) name *yĕhûd* appearing on the coins of the sub-province of Judah when they began to be minted,[27] as well as on seals and jar handle stamps of the period.[28] This means that we must distinguish between the cultic congregation, the *qĕhal yiśrā'ēl*, and the province of Judah and its peoples in discussions of the post-exilic community. The two are not identical, as J. P. Weinberg had demonstrated.[29] By this period, the name Israel is restricted to the cultic community, which, in a few instances, could include the Jews of the Diaspora who shared the same religious concepts which had been forged in the exilic communities of Babylonia.[30]

The exclusionistic tendencies of the *gōlāh* community appear to have emerged soon after the return to Judah, as can be seen from the events surrounding the rebuilding of the temple in Jerusalem. Details about the initial attempt to rebuild under Sheshbazzar are incomplete and somewhat confused, probably because of telescoping.[31] Ezra claims that the work halted with only the altar and foundation wall in place (3:1–10) because of a confrontation with the "people of

[26] This phrase does not occur in the book of Nehemiah, which may indicate that he preceded Ezra. It also indicates that Nehemiah dealt mainly with administrative matters, according to Mowinckel, *Studien zu dem Buche Ezra-Nehemia* I, 85.

[27] See B. Kanael, "Ancient Jewish Coins and their Historical Importance," *BA* 26 (1963) 38–62. On the obverse side of a coin of the Persian period there is "a male divinity, bearded . . . seated on a winged wheel," (p. 40). This could indicate that the Jewish society of the later Persian period was not yet "free" from iconography.

[28] See, for instance, Stern, *Material Culture of the Land of the Bible in the Persian Period*, 210ff.

[29] He calls the cultic congregation the "Bürger-Tempel-Gemeinde" (J. P. Weinberg, "Demographische Notizen zur Geschichte der nachexilischen Gemeinde in Juda," *Klio* 54 [1972] 45–58).

[30] Cf. the discussion of Joshua 22, p. 109, n. 23 above.

[31] For the presence of telescoping in the texts and attempts to reconstruct the sequence of events, see, for instance, Ackroyd, "Historical Problems of the Early Achaemenian Period," 40ff.

the land" (4:4), the "adversaries of Judah and Benjamin" (4:1), who wanted to be included in the rebuilding efforts (4:1–5). No specifics are given, however, and an official accusation was only written against the *gōlāh* group in the days of Artaxerxes (4:7–22).[32] What is significant, in spite of the chronological problems, is the apparent exclusion of the local population from the rebuilding program in its various phases by the returned *gōlāh* community. This is consistent with their redefinition of the *qĕhal yiśrāʾēl* to include only the exilic community.

It is probable that the *gōlāh* group usurped the right to rebuild the temple which the Edict of Cyrus had granted to the people of the sub-province (*mĕdînāh*) of Judah at large, rather than to them specifically.[33] The edict, referred to in Ezra 6:3–5 (in Aramaic),[34] does not mention anything about permission being given to *return* to Judah; rather, it gives explicit permission to rebuild the temple, and orders the return of the temple vessels taken by Nebuchadrezzar.[35] This is consistent with Persian policy vis-à-vis subjugated

---

[32] F. C. Fensham sees Ezra 4:6–23 "as parenthetical." Its purpose is not to give a "chronological sequence," but rather to give us "the most important actions of the Samaritans against the Jews" (*The Books of Ezra and Nehemiah* [Grand Rapids, MI, 1982] 77).

[33] K. Galling concluded that the Cyrus edict only concerned the "Diaspora-Juden des Ostens" (*Studien zur Geschichte Israels im persischen Zeitalter*, 66).

[34] Cf. Meyer, *Die Entstehung des Judentums*, 8–12; M. Noth, *The History of Israel* (London, 1960) 306; R. de Vaux, "The Decrees of Cyrus and Darius on the Rebuilding of the Temple," in *The Bible and the Ancient Near East* (Garden City, NY, 1971) 63–96.

[35] The beginning of the Book of Ezra, of course, gives another picture of the meaning of the Cyrus edict (1:1–16). For the author of Ezra, the return was anchored in this edict; it inaugurated a new epoch. Therefore, there should be "a happy homecoming for those who had been deported and a speedy rebuilding of the temple" (Herrmann, *A History of Israel*, 299). The presentation of Cyrus as the one who makes the plans for the temple's rebuilding should be compared with the Chronicler's presentation of David as the architect of the Solomonic temple, cf. Bright, *A History of Israel*, 361. David and Cyrus were both builders of empires which inaugurated new epochs. Therefore, both began by building the temple, the symbol of the god's kingdom on earth, i.e., the state.

peoples,[36] which acknowledged their status as "nations" under Persian rule by granting them the right to rebuild their official temples. The recognition and reorganization of religion and cult was part of an orderly administration because religion was a form of legal and administrative organization which regulated life. Religion expressed the divine order as codified in the *dat*, 'law.' This word is used to describe Ezra's law in Ezra 7:12.[37] By excluding the local population of the province from participating in the rebuilding of the temple, the *gōlāh* group was usurping the right of the entire territory of Judah,[38] thereby setting themselves up as the new religious and political leaders of the province.[39]

[36] For the attitude of the Persians toward the religions of subjugated peoples, see, among others, H. S. Nyberg, "Das Reich der Achämeniden," *Historia Mundi* III (Bern, 1954) 95f.; A. T. Olmstead, *History of the Persian Empire* (Chicago and London, 1948) 119f., 465.

[37] Cf. G. Widengren, "Iran and Israel in Parthian Times with Special Regard to the Ethiopic Book of Enoch," in *Religious Syncretism in Antiquity* (ed. B. A. Pearson; Missoula, MT, 1975) 89. It is thus conceivable that Persian influences affected early Judaism through the law of Ezra.

[38] Sheshbazzar was probably in charge of returning the temple vessels to Jerusalem. In Ezra 5:14, he bears the title *peḥāh*, "governor," and is commanded by Cyrus to go to Jerusalem with the temple vessels. His appointment as *hannāśîʾ līyhûdāh*, 'the chief for Judah,' (Ezra 1:7–11) does not require him to have been a prince of Judah, as most scholars have envisioned him. The prepositional *lamed* is not a genitive here. Sheshbazzar was probably a Babylonian official in the service of the new rulers. The Hebrew term "means a person raised to a position of authority and nothing more" (Fensham, *The Books of Ezra and Nehemiah*, 46). Cf G. W. Ahlström, "Some Aspects of Historical Problems in the Early Persian Period," *Eastern Great Lakes Biblical Society/Proceedings* IV (Westerville, OH, 1984) 57ff.

[39] This may have caused some priests and some of the local population to move to the North out of the jurisdiction of the *gōlāh* leaders. Neh 13:28f., for instance, states that Nehemiah forced a grandson of the high priest Eliashib to leave Jerusalem and Judah because he had married a daughter of Sanballat, the governor of the sub-province of Samerina. Josephus mentions that several priests and "Israelites" had married women from the province of Samerina (*Antiq.* XI, 312; cf. F. M. Cross, "A Reconstruction of the Judean Restoration," *JBL* 94 [1975] 5f.). Herrmann maintains that the ones who had "entered into such marriages were

They successfully secured their position with the arrival of Ezra and the law scroll which had official Persian recognition as the new law of the province (Ezra 7:26). The new law had to be accepted by everyone who wanted to be counted as a member of the (new) society, i.e., the society of Yahweh's people, the "real" Israel. It almost certainly was written by members of the exilic community who were still outside of Judah, but who shared the theological views of the returned *gōlāh* community which had evolved during the Exile. The fact that the law was in Ezra's hand before he left for Judah (7:14)[40] clearly demonstrates that the law scroll was not at home in Jerusalem, even though it was meant to be normative for the Judean society and all Yahweh worshipers in Palestine including, theoretically, the "Samaritans."[41]

The law scroll was not necessarily a new set of statutes. Many old laws which had been known to the leaders of the Diaspora could have been incorporated in their old form, or

---

chiefly the upper classes. . . . The marriages probably represented an attempt by the upper class to improve their position by entering into relations with their counterparts in neighboring countries" (*A History of Israel*, 307). This kind of "exodus" to the North where they could continue to worship Yahweh would have intensified the religious propaganda produced by both North and South. The North could once again claim to be the people of Yahweh, i.e., Israel, as the Samaritans still do. For the history and early development of this northern Yahwism leading to the Samaritan-Jewish conflict, see, among others, J. D. Purvis, *The Samaritan Pentateuch and the Origins of the Samaritan Sect* (Harvard Semitic Monogr. 2; Cambridge, MA, 1968); R. J. Coggins, *Samaritans and Jews: The Origins of Samaritanism Reconsidered* (Oxford, 1975); H. G. Kippenberg, *Garizim und Synagoge: Traditionsgeschichtliche Untersuchungen zur samaritanischen Religion der aramäische Periode* (Berlin, 1971) 33–171.

[40] For the depiction of Ezra as a second Moses, cf. K. Koch, "Ezra and the Origin of Judaism," *JSS* 19 (1974) 187.

[41] Cf. H. Cazelles, "La mission d'Esdras," *VT* 4 (1954) 130f. A. T. Olmstead understood Ezra's mission in Jerusalem as "a new project for Jewish colonization," which had been authorized by the Persian king (*History of Palestine and Syria* [New York and London, 1931] 583). The characterization of Ezra as a "scribe skilled in the law of Moses" may be an attempt by the narrator to avoid explaining how a new law had been "revealed" in the time of Ezra, cf. Koch, "Ezra and the Origin of Judaism," 181f.

perhaps, in a somewhat modified form. Since, however, the people of Jerusalem did not know this law and the priests and Levites had to learn it before teaching it to the people, parts of the scroll must have been new (Neh 8:7, 13). The new, unfamiliar parts can probably be attributed to two sources: the Persian court and the exilic *gōlāh* party which produced the document. The Persians would have made sure that the laws of the different provinces and sub-provinces were acceptable to the Persian court. By modifying the area's old law code and then reinstating it as the former law of the 'God of the Heavens,' *ʾēlāh šēmayyāh* (Ezra 7:23), they could impose their will on the province of Judah while maintaining friendly relations.[42] The *gōlāh* party, on the other hand, was able to "institutionalize" the sectarian precepts which had developed during the Exile and make them normative for the entire Judean society by including them in the officially sanctioned scroll. Included here, for instance, were laws prohibiting mixed marriages (Ezra 10:7f.) and new rules concerning the cultic calendar.[43]

[42] J. G. Vink has proposed that one of the goals of Ezra's mission was "a strengthening of the ties between the Persian court and the Palestinian community" ("The Date and Origin of the Priestly Code in the Old Testament," 139, cf. 39). The title "God of the Heavens" may have been used by the exiled peoples in their contacts with the Persian court. A. Vincent thought the title was used for political reasons, even if it might have had its roots in old Israelite society, and that it was similar to titles used to describe Ahura Mazda (*La religion judéo-araméenes d'Éléphantine* [Paris, 1937] 142). While this title is not found in Persian royal inscriptions, its origin may still be "sought in the diplomatic terminology of the Persian administration," according to D. K. Andrews. He thinks that the title might have been "used by government officials to evaluate the deities of subject peoples and relate them to Ahura Mazda" ("Yahweh and the God of Heavens," *The Seed of Wisdom: Essays in Honour of T. J. Meek* [ed. W. S. McCullough; Toronto, 1964] 52).

[43] One of the new statutes informed the people that for the festival in the seventh month, they had to go out into the hills and bring back branches of olives, palms, and myrtle to build booths in which to dwell during the festival, "as Moses had told them"(!) (Neh 8:14–17). This is an example of the attempt to authorize a new law by linking it with the name of Moses. As discussed earlier in chap. V, pp. 47ff., the Passover legislation probably was formulated and promulgated at this time, linking

After Ezra arrived with the new law scroll, the inhabitants of the territory of Judah apparently were assembled in Jerusalem to accept the scroll as the official law of the province. The Book of Ezra reports this event in terms of the assembling of members of the *gōlāh* community only, thereby ignoring the existence of the people of the land who were not members of his party and who did not share his goals and theological outlook (10:7–8). For him, then, only members of the people of Yahweh, Israel, were concerned with the law which regulated the new society. We may safely assume, however, that all citizens of the sub-province of Judah would have been required to attend to official presentation of the new law and swear their allegiance to it, thereby indicating their loyalty to their Persian overlord. It is possible that the threat of land confiscation for non-attendance which is made to the *gōlāh* community in 10:7 originally was leveled against all residents of the province.

The description of the presentation of the law scroll, described in the Book of Ezra, signals the beginning of Judaism. Those members of the *gōlāh* community who failed to accept the new law were to be excluded from the assembly of the captivity, the *qĕhal haggôlāh*, i.e., the people of Yahweh, Israel. Never before could a person have been excluded from a society because of marriage, for instance. Such a society had not existed in the Near East prior to the time of Ezra. Those who did not accept the laws of Ezra[44]

---

the old festival of *maṣṣôt* with the Exodus narrative to create a new festival. See also E. Kutsch, "Erwägungen zur Geschichte der Passahfeier und des Massotfestes," *Zeitschrift für Theologie und Kirche* 55 (1958) 1ff.

[44] The issue of whether the law of Ezra is identical with parts of the Pentateuch cannot be solved here. Much of the material in the *tōrāh* writings must have been included in the stipulations in Ezra's law. J. M. Myers, among others, has maintained that "Ezra's lawbook, so far as it can be checked, seems to have corresponded closely to the legal materials in our present Pentateuch" (*Ezra and Nehemiah* [Anchor Bible 14; Garden City, NY, 1965] lxii). It is logical that laws which were "canonized" by later Judaism would have been in harmony with the founder of the movement. We may assume that the Pentateuchal books were edited in the period after Ezra, when they received their present form. E. Rivkin thinks that the Pentateuch was a successful attempt by the Aaronides "to rescue

never became part of the new society, the new Israel, even people who had belonged to the groups which had returned from Babylonia. Thus, we have an even further narrowing of the *qĕhal yiśrā'ēl* in the book of Ezra which "weeded out" unfaithful members of the *gōlāh* flock. These people never became Jews! They were still Judahites, however, along with a large portion of the local population of the sub-province— a phenomenon usually neglected in the treatments of the history of Judah and its peoples.

We can conclude from the foregoing discussion that the name Israel, when used as a religious designation of the cultic community of Yahweh, underwent a process of development after the destruction of the Israelite kingdom in 722 B.C. Beginning as a description which could be applied to Yahweh worshipers of both Israel and Judah, it came to be restricted to the cultic community of the state of Judah, and was further narrowed after the fall of the state of Judah to members of the communities which had been exiled from the land of Judah. As a final step, it became the ideological name for those who accepted the Babylonian-Persian party's religious laws and customs. All other Judahites who worshiped Yahweh, including the Samaritans, were excluded from membership in Yahweh's people Israel in the writings of the leaders of the new society in Jerusalem. Membership in this society was not based on political, civil, or territorial considerations; it was dependent upon embracing this new religious, "Mosaic" law of Ezra, the law which made one a member of the people of God.[45]

Yahwism from deterioration and extinction," under their leadership of Yahweh's people (*The Shaping of Jewish History: A Radical New Interpretation* [New York, 1971] 34). We should note while discussing this issue that S. Mowinckel considered the *qāhāl* theology to be proof of a post-exilic date for D, which he labeled a "Konstitutionsbuch" for the restored, post-exilic community (*Ezra-Nehemiah* I, 90). Cf. S. A. Kaufman, who also maintains that the "Law of Deuteronomy" (Deuteronomy 12–26) is a "program of politico-religious centralization." He is more inclined to connect it with the Josianic period ("The Structure of the Deuteronomic Law," *Maarav* 1 [1978–79] 147).

[45] The ideological use of the term Israel continued in the Qumran community, "the right Israel," (1QS i 22f.; viii 9 etc.) and in the early

A short summary of the results of this investigation would be that from its very beginning, the name Israel, as far as is known, was a territorial term linked to the central hill country of Palestine. As a consequence, all settlers of the hills could be labeled Israelites. This means that the Israelite societies and their culture were an integral part of the Canaanite scene and should be seen as a continuation of the Late Bronze traditions rather than as intrusive. When a territorial state later emerged in this part of the country under Saul's leadership, the name of the territory naturally became the name for this new nation. Thus, the name Israel first became a political designation at that time. After the split of the United Monarchy, Israel continued as a name for the northern kingdom. This political significance of the name came to an end when Israel became an Assyrian province under the name Samerina. After that time, Israel no longer referred to a political entity. The name Israel still lived on, however, as a religious, ideal name for Yahweh's people. In the liturgies of the United Monarchy Israel signified the *qāhāl*, the cult congregation, of Yahweh. It continued to be used in this way in the southern kingdom, Judah. Some Jerusalemite groups seem to have emphasized that Judah was the remnant of the people of Yahweh, *de facto* Yahweh's people, a concept which lived on through the Exile and into the post-exilic period. In the last period, however, the name underwent a further narrowing in meaning. It became the term for the new Yahweh society which emerged within the party of the returnees, the *gōlāh*, and particularly after Ezra's arrival with the new law. At that point Israel became an ideological term for Judaism.

Christian church, i.e., "the new Israel," or as Gal 6:16 expresses it, "Israel of God." Both illustrate how a term could continue to be redefined by different groups in different ways over the course of time.

Index of Authors

Subject Index

Aaron 37
Aaronides 116
Abdi-Ashirta 14, 16, 24
Abdi-Hepa 66f.
Abdon 77
Abib 51
Abimelech 16, 66f., 69, 71, 78
Abner 94
ᶜbr 15
Abraham 89, 108
Abydos 63
Achish 18
Adam 23
ᵓadāmāh 93
adamātu 93
Adoram 98
Aegyptos 61
ᶜAfula 29, 69
Ahura Mazda 115
Ai 27, 29
Aijalon 60, 64
ᶜal 88
Alalakh 12, 87f.
ᶜly 78
ᶜam 87
ᶜam hā ᵓāreṣ 105
Amada Stele 38
Amalek(ites) 34f., 57, 90, 92
ᶜAmarah 60
Amarna 2f., 9, 13, 15ff., 18, 24,
    40, 66
Amaᵓu 87

Amenhotep II 12, 45, 66
Amenhotep III 89
Ammia 16
Ammon(ites) 11, 18, 57f., 85f., 90,
    92, 96, 103f., 106
Amon 17
Amorites 11, 61, 64, 71, 76, 82,
    106
Amphictyony 8
Amuq 36
Amurru 14, 24
ᵓan 62
Anath 59
Anatolia 36, 62
Andromeda 62
ᵓnywt 62
Aphek 4, 23, 29, 31
ᶜapīru 11ff., 14ff., 17f., 31, 37, 66f.
Aqabah 99
Arabah 58
Arabs 89f., 104
Arad 34
ᵓărammi 17
Arameans 11, 17, 36, 70, 82, 92,
    96
Ark of Yahweh 74, 93
Artaxerxes 112
Asher 11, 62ff., 88f., 95
Asherah 7, 58, 93
Ashkelon 38, 61
Ashtartu 59
Ashur (Assyria) 42, 59, 89f., 110

Index of Passages

Colophon

Designed by David C. Baker.
Input by Barbara J. Manahan.
Set in Palatino on a Varityper 5900 photo-typesetter by James E. Eisenbraun.
Layout by Dana L. Williamson.
Maps prepared by Paul R. Mattson.
Dustjacket design by David French.
Production supervised by David L. Zapf.
Printed on 60# Glatfelter Natural by Braun-Brumfield, Ann Arbor, MI.

DATE	ISSUED TO

DEMCO